THE LIFE OF ST SHENOUDA

Translation of The Arabic Life

By: Abba Wissa

THE LIFE OF ST SHENOUDA

Translation of The Arabic Life

BY: ABBA WISSA

(from Amelineau's edition)

ST SHENOUDA'S MONASTERY

SYDNEY, AUSTRALIA

2015

The Life of St Shenouda
Translation of The Arabic Life

ST SHENOUDA MONASTERY
8419, Putty Rd,
Putty, NSW, 2330
Australia

www.stshenoudamonastery.org.au

ISBN 13: 978-0-9941910-6-9

Cover Design:
Sandra Bottros

Cover Illustration:
Icon of St Shenouda from St Anthony's Monastery, Red Sea

Contents

Publisher's Introduction

St Shenouda is one of the fifth century's most renowned Egyptian monastic leaders. During his monastic leadership his community grew to around four thousand monks and nuns. His spiritual ministry and miraculous works extended beyond the walls of his monastery to surrounding villages. He is known for his large library of Coptic Christian writings that are scattered today in museums and libraries all over the world.

He did not gain much attention from the western writers of the time such as Jerome, Palladius, and John Cassian, because of his patriotism to the Coptic language and culture which dissociated him from many Greek and Latin writers.

His life comes to us in Coptic in both dialects, Sahidic and Bohairic. This translation of the Arabic life of St Shenouda is from the edition by the French Coptologiest Amelineau. It is believed that this Arabic life is a translation from the Sahidic Coptic life, sometime in the seventh century.

This is the first translation of the Arabic Life made in the English language. The Chapter headings are an addition made by the publisher to make the text more reader friendly.

Introduction

In the Name of the Father, the Son and the Holy Spirit, one God Amen.

With the help of God and by His grace we begin to record the sayings of our father the perfect and great saint, the pure star St. Abba Wissa in honour of the great St. Abba Shenouda the Archimandrite in the mountain of Atribe of the desert of Thebes, in the peace of the Lord. Amen.

The Orthodox Christians who resided in the villages of Qaou, Akhmim and Absai gathered together after the departure of the great St. Shenouda to visit our father St. Wissa to comfort him. This they did to offer their condolences because of the saint's departure, which the Lord, to whom is blessing and glory, had caused to happen, after He had entrusted St. Wissa with the same rank as our father St. Shenouda.

When the congregation; those who lived in nearby monasteries, and those who were in communion with St. Wissa in monasticism heard about his righteousness in worship, gracefulness and the wisdom of God in him, they called out saying, "Our Father! The place of the fathers has been given to the children. You deserve the status of St. Shenouda the Archimandrite. At which point they asked him saying; "We want to be hydrated from the spring of your holy blessings for the sheep are always cared for by the shepherd". When he saw the constant longing for God in them and their enjoyment of listening to His words which are filled with grace and their wish to listen to the news of His servant, the righteous St. Shenouda, he consented. St. Wissa began to explain to them the wonders and miracles that God revealed through him for the glorification of God, for the benefit and gain of those who hear and apply them, to glorify God in every moment, who performs these wonders in His saints.

With the grace of God we will now begin with the sayings of St. Wissa.

The Sayings Of St Shenouda

This was said by St. Wissa on the commemoration of St. Shenouda on the 7th of Abib:

"Welcome people, lovers of Christ, especially the monastic fathers who carry out God's commands and the teachings of my elder and pure father which are soothing to the soul. Make use of this blessing and be enriched by his love. Everyone, listen to me carefully and contemplate as I start to talk about the wonders and miracles that God has performed through the hands of our pure and blessed father St. Shenouda whom I, Wissa, his son and disciple have witnessed and those that were spoken to me by his own mouth without lie or fault, these of which I narrate to you now.

St. Shenouda used to always teach saying that there are two paths, one to life and the other to death. There is a great difference between these two paths. The path to life is to love the Lord your God above all else with all your heart, all your spirit and all your mind and to love your neighbour as you do yourself and with all your mind. Do not do to others what you would not accept for yourself. Do these deeds one by one; first, do not kill, commit fornication nor defile yourself by loving something unclean. Do not be corrupt, steal, perform witchcraft nor provide a pregnant woman with medication to perform abortion and do not kill her new born.

Do not desire what is your friend's or neighbour's. Do not swear with a lie and do not speak evil about another person lest the Lord become angry at you and be careful not to be of two minds in all you do. Do not speak lies or useless words. Do not reduce the pay of a worker lest they implore the Lord and He listens to them, because indeed our Lord is near us my son. Do not snatch, extort, be a loan shark or falsify with evil. Do not be arrogant, because the arrogant is despised by God. Do not speak in a bad manner about your friend, neighbour or adversary for God may favour them more than you my son. Do not abuse anyone, because they are in the image of God. If someone stumbled and fell in sin reproach them in private. If you are in charge of a group, love them as you would yourself. Escape from all evil and do not mingle with evil doers lest your age become limited and you die not in accordance with God's plan for you my son.

Do not be envious, hateful or imperious because all these teach a person to kill. Do not endeavour in lusts because lust leads to fornication. Do not speak ridicule or let your eye be greedy lest they make a false witness. Do not ask for a sign or a miracle, this may lead to worshiping of idols. Do not watch time because woes, wailing, worries and hesitation descend upon those who do. Avoid fortune tellers or sorcerers or be close to or engage with them, because they can never be close to God. Do not be a liar because lying leads to theft. Do not love silver and do not gloat these will yield to murder. Do not be in despair and do not think in bad faith but be gentle for the gentle will inherit the earth.

My son, be noble, merciful with a simple heart. Be faithful in all good works. Always live in trembling and in the fear of God's word. Do not be even a little lofty with yourself, but always be humble. Do not be contiguous with the rich, but associate with the righteous and the humble, because by humility David the prophet was saved. Be grateful for the good and evil that befalls you and learn that nothing will occur to you without the Lord's permission.

My son, remember God's words in your heart, at night and during the day because the Lord is present wherever His name is remembered and He is worthy of honour and praise forever. Always tread in purity. Do not seek to oppose nor quarrel with your fellow brothers, but seek to resolve disputes. Judge with fairness and do not consider it inappropriate to reproach the wrong doers for their wrong doing and the sinners for their sin.

My son, take heed that you do not extend your hand in haste to take and yet retract when giving. Give to the poor as long as you can afford, in order to gain forgiveness of your many sins. Do not be of two hearts when giving, and if you give, do not be upset or regret that you acted mercifully. Remember that the honest and good judge is the Lord, the forgiver of sins. Do not turn away from a poor man, but give him as much as you can afford. Share in the sorrow of the sad and the poor. If we share with those who do not have this life's perishables, we will certainly share with them then in the everlasting.

If we carry out these commandments we will tread in the path of life and the blessed course forever, which is for the one King our Lord Jesus Christ who is generous towards those who seek Him.

As for the path of death and those who tread its course, they will die a horrible death because of all their evil deeds. These deeds involve cursing, murder, stealing, hypocrisy and every evil act we have just described. All who do these are the ones who fall in the path of death and tread its ways by performing evil deeds.

Prophecies Concerning His Birth

These teachings which our father St. Shenouda used to always teach us I have now described to you O people of God. I will now talk of some of the many miracles and wonders that God has performed through His saint, St. Shenouda. Lately, I have been burdened and troubled since I am feeble and unskilled in speaking. I am afraid to go into the wondrous works of my father St. Shenouda lest I be plunged into the waters of the sea without knowing how to swim. Although I owe a great deal, the creditor is not concerned for these things, for my father St. Shenouda is worthy of his good works related, and also his asceticism, his way of life, his admirable virtues and the great and incredible signs just like those of the holy prophets and the apostles of the Lord.

Our father and great prophet St. Shenouda was from a village called Shandawil from the surroundings of Akhmim. There was a time when the mother of this saint went to fill up water and along the way met with certain brethren who were travelling north undertaking an important errand for their monastery. Accompanying them was Fr. Horesios who when he saw her, came down from his ride, kissed her head three times and blessed her saying "The Lord will grow good fruit from you and his name will be remembered forever".

The brethren with him were astonished and said "Father, scarcely do you allow yourself to look at a woman, so what happened today?" He replied to them "Glory be to God my brothers and children, for from this woman will come a grain of salt enlightening to the whole world." One of the brethren who was wise and knowledgeable among them, whom the father always consulted because he was of good opinion, said "Glory be to God, my father. When you approached the lady I saw an angel of God carrying a sword in his hand surrounding her. When you kissed her head, the angel spoke to you saying, "Peace be with you beloved of God. The one to come from her will repose many hearts and God will speak with him frequently." Father Hirsasios replied "Yes, I saw my son. The angel accompanies her so that the evil one may not find a place in her till she gives birth to the boy and feeds him from her milk." He continued "Glory be to our God forever. God has raised for us a pure saint" And another said "God has blessed our generation".

We were also informed of another amazing witness. When the heretics were fighting our beloved father the patriarch St. Athanasius the Apostolic he spoke by what was written saying "For the weapons of our warfare are not carnal but mighty in God for pulling down strongholds". He headed north till he reached the city of Akhmim, visiting cities and villages and praying there. There was a pagan temple in the city called Metros where many people were led to destruction within it. Now the

Lord, blessed be His name, chose to visit and comfort him.

At midnight, when he had heard of this famed terror in this wilderness, he rose up immediately. Now the Archangel Michael appeared to him in glory saying "Peace be with you. The peace of our Lord Jesus Christ be with you the rest of your days. Do not be afraid for I am near to you. Follow me that I may show you the power of our Lord along with the prayers of the saints and your pleadings." The angel took him next to the temple and said to him, "spread your arms in the shape of the cross that you may see and be amazed." Immediately the angel drew a sword of fire and extended his hand over the four corners of the temple and it was demolished to the ground and the fire burnt all impurities within it. Immediately he lifted his hands towards heaven and gave thanks to God saying "You my Lord are righteous and Your laws are perfect forever, O You the good bridegroom. You have rightly judged this city O Lord of heaven and earth". He then knelt to the Archangel Michael saying "I rejoice at your arrival today in my exiled state for you have shown great mercy towards me."

The Archangel said to the patriarch, "It is well O lover of saints. Listen to me for I will inform you of what will become of you. The people of your city will come to you here after three days. They will confess that you are the good shepherd and they will praise and honour you. You will teach them the words of the Lord when they affirm and highly revere you, O father of the whole world. After that, they will carry you to Alexandria and the people of your city will go out to welcome you saying, "Your coming to us is truly good. We are rejoiced by your arrival O you the good shepherd of all the regions of Egypt"

"The heretics will then hear of you and the gifts which God has performed through you. One by one they will know you, but on the day in which God will seat you on your seat, a boy will be born in the village of Shandawil. His name will be Shenouda, meaning 'the son of God.'" He will be born on the seventh of Bashans. When he is born, your spirit will double on him for he is worthy of it and has been worthy with the prophet Elijah in that time where Elijah's spirit doubled on Elisha the prophet. The place in which the boy will be born will become a venerable church. He will be renowned and all the kings will come to know about his wonders and miracles. He will fulfil the prophecies of saints and in his days many heretics will disappear and many people will be saved by his hands. In his monastery will be a great and continuous recitation and I will appear to him many times, I will Comfort him for his perseverance and pains. He will be great like all the saints by his honesty, love, peace and patience. People will receive him as they do a father, brother and lover. The Virgin, the mother of God, will call him my Son's beloved. His seed will remain forever. Peace to you, be saved by the power of the Holy Trinity."

This which I have explained to you my beloved is what I have known from my saintly fathers.

We shall now return and reveal to you the story of his father.

His father was called Abgous and as we have heard and learnt from his parents, he became a monk and was promoted to Hegumen here. Thus we asked his father about the righteous of St. Shenouda and he told us his miracles and wonders, which he performed since his childhood and said;

"His mother and I were in deep sorrow and without comfort for we did not have a child to fill our life with joy. For truly, the joy and pleasure of man is in his seed. One day I saw a vision at night, as if a star had shone into my house and I was astonished for I had never witnessed anything like it except for the morning and evening stars. I heard a voice saying to me, while I was in bed, that this star will shine upon your son the day he is born and will shine onto his monastery till the end of the world. This I heard three times.

While I was in the midst of this vision, his mother woke me and told me what she had seen. She said, "I saw a vision where there was a lady standing by my head saying to me "Peace to you Darouba." I looked up and saw a cross in her hand. She gave me a loaf of bread and I said to her "Who are you my lady?" She replied, "Since the day the man of God kissed your head and blessed you, I and those with me asked God that his angel keep a shining sword with him always to keep the devil away from you until this good fruit is born from you. The time is near and there will be complete joy for you. Now you will call his name Shenouda, for I will be his companion forever. When he departs, his monastery will have a great reputation and many people will come from everywhere. Many monks will keep his commandments forever. Therefore be careful not to use any harmful food or nourishment until he is weaned from your milk and he will intercede for you and his father. Be strong in God and let the glory of God be with you forever"

Thus this amazing news I have revealed to you O beloved of Christ.

His Childhood

His father the blessed elder Abgous said that it was all fulfilled. It was the Seventh of Bashans when he was born and we made a great feast and there was great joy. The young boy Shenouda had then begun to grow up in the grace of God which was in him and was gradually becoming more and more attractive.

This blessed man, the father of this saint was a farmer who had a small flock that he appointed to someone else to look after. The shepherd said to the father "Give me your boy Shenouda to watch over the sheep with me and in return I will give a little of my wages for him. Please have compassion on me and help me."

When they saw that the shepherd's heart was intent, the mother said to him: "I will give my son to you but send him back to me at evening of each day. He is my only son and I rejoice to God with him night and day." The shepherd answered and said to them "Every day before the sun sets I will send him back to you" So henceforth, the shepherd took the boy St. Shenouda to shepherd the sheep with him and each day when evening came, before sunset, the shepherd would send the saint back to his home in the village. However St. Shenouda, once he was dismissed, used to go down to a lake not far from the village and stretch out his hands to pray. The water would come up to his neck till morning arrived.

The mother and father used to get upset with the Shepherd every day saying to him "why did you not send the boy in the evening to the village. Do you not realise that we worry about him lest any harm come to him during his absence with you?" The shepherd replied "Truly, I do send him back to you every evening" On one of these days then, the shepherd sent off the boy and followed him until he reached the lake. Overlooking the lake was a sycamore tree. The boy went down to the water and there spread his hands and prayed to God saying "Lord, I thank you, manage my life as you wish". The shepherd remained hidden behind the sycamore tree in order to see what the boy would do.

The shepherd would often testify and say "I saw the fingers of the boy light up like ten flaming lamps! Then I smelt a great fragrance and such a supreme perfume I have never smelt before. I then returned to the sheep until morning." When it was morning his father came and was upset with me and said "why did you not send me my son back to me at evening?" I said to him, "Take your son with you. I am not worthy to have him stay with me" This is what the shepherd told us when he testified to us.

The father took the boy to his house and informed his mother of all that had happened. After ten days he took

him and went to the monastery to receive a blessing from
Abba Pigol. It happened that on that day a number of high
ranked people and leaders of Akhmim were congregating
at the monastery and Abba Pigol was teaching and guiding
them for the salvation of their souls. When the father and
the boy were about a mile away from them, Abba Pigol got
up and said to those seated with him "Let us rise and meet
the Archimandrite, the abbot of the monastery, for he is
nearby." He and those with him rose and went out to meet
the boy with his father. Abba Pigol took the hand of the boy
and placed it on his head and said "Bless me O my father
and Archimandrite." Then he said to those walking with
him "This is the promise and covenant of God in my hand."

When they entered and sat, there was a man possessed by
an unclean spirit who was sitting near Abba Pigol. When
the boy, St. Shenouda, saw the spirit which was in the man
he stretched out his hand, seized a small board and began
to beat the demon which was in the man. The evil spirit
cried out saying "I will flee from your face O Shenouda, for
truly from the time I saw you, fire has devoured me." From
that very moment, the spirit departed from the man and he
regained his health and gave glory to God. Abba Pigol said
to the young boy Shenouda "Wait until the time comes my
son."

After these events, Abba Pigol spoke with his father and said
"Let the young boy stay with me this week till I examine
him and learn what the Lord will make of him for I am very
pleased with him." Because St. Shenouda's mother was the
sister of Abba Pigol (from the same mother and father), they
joyfully left the boy with his uncle. At evening of that day,

Anba Pigol laid down by himself in a certain place and the boy laid down by himself in another place.

When Abba Pigol raised his eyes up to heaven he saw an angel of the Lord guarding the young boy Shenouda while he was sleeping. The angel said to Abba Pigol "When you wake up in the morning you will find next to Shenouda an Eskeem (A leather belt of crosses worn by monks), put it on him for it is the belt of Elijah the Tishbite which the Lord Jesus has sent to you to put upon him. Truly he will be a righteous and illustrious man and after him no one like him will arise in any country. He will build a monastery and to everyone he enters his place, he will be a comfort and protection. His community will endure for all generations."

When Abba Pigol arose in the morning, he took the belt which he found before him, called St. Shenouda and put it upon him. Having made him a monk, he kept him with him. A few days after this when they were dwelling together, Abba Pigol and the young man Shenouda went out walking together and with them also went Abba Bishay, from Mount Epsoi (modern day Red Monastery). He too was a holy man who walked after Godly things. When these three were walking together, there came to them a voice from heaven saying "Today Shenouda was appointed Archimandrite of the whole world. Abba Pigol said to Abba Bishay "My brother, did you too hear this voice, which came from heaven?" Abba Bishay replied "Indeed I did." When they had agreed between them as to what they had heard Abba Pigol said to Abba Bishay "Let us ask the young boy Shenouda aswell." So they asked him "Did you hear this voice crying out from heaven?" He answered confirming them saying "Yes, indeed I heard." Abba Pigol said to him "What was it that you heard?" To which he answered "I heard the voice saying, 'today Shenouda was appointed Archimandrite of the whole world.'" Abba Pigol and Abba Bishay were greatly astonished and glorified God saying "Truly he will be perfect".

When the holy father St. Shenouda had received the angelic garment which came to him from heaven, he gave himself up to the anchoritic life with many great labours, many nocturnal vigils and fasts without number. Nor did he break his fast until the sun had set in the evening, even then he would not eat to fill himself. His body, therefore, became weak and his flesh was stuck to his bones. His food was bread, salt and water only, thus resembling our father Elijah the Tishbite in all his days.

His Way of Life

In this way as he was always so zealous in his labours, he was a teacher of all. Not only of the young but also of the old. He bore Christ, persevering in the recitation of the scriptures and as a consequence, his renown and his teachings were sweet in everyone's mouths like honey to the heart of those who seek to love eternal life. He would deliver many sermons and discourses full of holy precepts. He established rules for the monks and wrote beneficial letters and brought both fear and comfort to the souls of men. Of everything which came from his mouth he said "No word that I utter comes from myself alone, there is none which Christ does not deliver to me." He adorned his life gloriously with the perfection of monastic labours, great asceticism and a multitude of ascetic practises. He placed laws for his children the monks and for other saintly monks not under his discipleship. He documented many sayings filled with reproachful words concerning the moment when the human soul departs and exits the body.

A group from Alexandria took a book of the Sayings of our father the saint and went with it to the bodies of the apostles

Peter and Paul in Rome. It was to Peter that the Lord Christ had said "your eyes will not turn away from the light of this world forever"

The whole body of Peter was shrouded except for his face as the Lord had said. When they put the book forward to the bodies of the pure apostles, the apostle pulled out his hand from the shroud, held it and kissed it three times and said "We welcome your arrival here today our lover, the teacher and pure apostle. The teacher Paul became the thirteenth disciple and you are the fourteenth. You sit and judge your disciple monks because the saints have presented you and deemed you fit for it."

When people had heard this, they glorified God for what the pure apostles had spoken regarding the teachings of my father the saint. Many people glorified God and his saints because of what they witnessed and what had occurred in the great city of Rome.

The Lord was always with him in all his days. When he was in his monastery, he would see a multitude of sins being committed throughout the whole world. And of those who came to him, he would know all that they had thought and done. He would therefore pray for them all so that they may be saved and find mercy at the judgement of Christ.

On a certain Friday, he worked a piece of wood into a cross and tied himself to it. He stood with his hands open in the shape of a cross and he remained in that state until the end of the week. He used to do that in order to suffer with his

Master and to crucify his organs. His virtues were many, too numerous to recite and so were the hardships of his worship since his youth until he was of good age.

He lived a whole month on half a loaf of bread dipped in salt. He completed his monastic life in great asceticism and countless prayer. He would pray twelve times a day, making twenty four prostrations each time. At night, he would not sleep at all until day break. Afterwards, for the sake of the body, he would sleep just a little so that it would not perish too quickly. There were many times where he did not eat from Saturday to Saturday. And again for the forty days of Holy Easter he would not eat bread. His food instead was edible vegetables and moistened grain. As a result of this, there was hardly any flesh on him. Tears to him were sweet as honey and because of the great flow of tears continually flowing, his eyes were deeply sunken like holes in walls.

The Devil Appears to Him

One day while he was sitting in his cave in the desert working with his hands, the devil appeared to him in the form of an angel of God. The devil entered to the righteous man and said to him "Peace be to you O good young man. The Lord has sent me to comfort you, therefore, cease this asceticism and poverty, and move from this desert to the villages. Eat your bread with your brothers for the Lord has said, "With long life I will satisfy you", but in these sufferings you will die before your age is complete"

When my father heard that, he immediately realised that it was the enemy and said to the devil "If you were an angel who came to comfort me, then spread your arms in the form of a cross so that we can pray to the Lord Jesus Christ". When the devil heard the name of the Lord Jesus Christ, his appearance changed to that of a beast with many great horns and he fought the saint. The saint resorted to his braid, which he had previously interweaved and tied the devil with it and hung him to a pole. The devil screamed a mighty scream that shook the mountain and he pleaded with the saint saying "I ask you not to perish me before my time."

My father said to him "I swear by the truths of the prayers of the saints if you return to this place again I will exile you to Babel of Chaldean till the great day of judgement." The saint released the devil and he left in great shame.

Our father St. Shenouda lived in the desert for five years and had not seen a grown field or grains in pots or the flooding of the Nile. He desired nothing of this world, nor to see or look at it on any day. One day Abba Ephraim came to him from the mountain of Repha. They greeted each other and sat and spoke about the wonders of God. This elder said to my father "You are great and your words are sweet O teacher, blessed is the womb that carried you and the breasts that fed you. Christ, the Lord, has granted you the gift of prophecy and your name reaches the ends of the earth. Your sayings reach unto every generation."

The Snares of the Devil

Fourteen miles away from the doorstep of my father St. Shenouda was a monk who found a water spring and rested by it. St. Shenouda informed us that this monk did not taste bread for nine years and he excelled over many of the ascetics. This monk used to hear the noise of the souls in torture and he used to speak face to face with angels. There was a time when a group of brethren went to him and said "The devil fights us and has caused us great pain." This great man said to them "The devil does not exist and I know nothing about the matter you enquired about." The group of monks departed in sadness for he did not supplicate to God and interceded on their behalf, but trusted in himself. One day, the devil took the form of a human king and with him a group of soldiers. They arrived at the residence of this monk and sat outside knocking at the door using large stones and called for him to exit quickly and so he did. While troubled, he found the king sitting surrounded by his soldiers. One of the soldiers presented the monk to the king and said "Our king is merciful and kind. He cares for the salvation of our souls. He does not care for the things of kings." The monk responded "What is this news?" The tormenter said "Since you have come out to us, no despair shall befall you and no evil will harm you. I am the king of the Edomites. The Persians attacked us and we were defeated and now we are here. Be kind to us and keep this girl with you until I go and face my enemy and if I do not return to you after a month of time know that the enemy was victorious and has defeated us at war. So show kindness to this girl and you will be rewarded greatly."

The girl cried and said "Do not be late father." They then left and the girl resided with the elder until the completion of the month and the monk did not know that she was from the army of the devil. She approached the monk and said "Know that my father has died and will not return again. Now have compassion on me and marry me and be my husband. I will be your lady and will take care of you. This will be far better than to expel me and let the wild animals devour me and eat my flesh at which point God will ask you to give account for me."

The monk heeded to the soft words of the girls, which were more bitter than cactus, and answered, "I cannot marry you, it is not appropriate for me to do so"; but the girl said, "I am your pride and glory". So the monk said, "Wait until I finish braiding this palm leaf and let it be according to God's will"

St. Shenouda knew about this great calamity through the Spirit as a result of the low standard which this monk reached because of the devil. So my father sighed and asked the Lord for the sake of this brother saying, "O Lord accept him and take him, so that he might be delivered from this evil temptation". When there was only one palm frond left, this brother fell on his back and submitted his spirit in the Lord's hands while holding the frond with his right hand.

My father said to Abba Aphram, "Let us go to bury Hercules the elder for he has departed now." They all walked while singing spiritual hymns until they reached his cell where they found him dead while holding one palm frond. My father said, "O Lord, You are Pious and Your laws are upright. You judged in justice because there would have been a great pain to occur if he had finished braiding this frond, as it is written a human being should not be proud of his glories".

They prayed then buried him and returned back safely. The angel of the Lord had spoken to my father and comforted him saying, "God our creator is merciful. He created us in His image and likeness. Go forth now and visit and comfort your children and those accompanying them." He came and informed us with what had happened.

A Blessing to Those Who Deserve It

A rich man called Peter from a country called Osim came seeking blessing from my father. He approached him saying, "Bless me my saintly father." My father answered, "You are not worthy for a blessing, you have committed a great sin when you married that woman who is your niece, and made this iniquity." So he answered, "My father, my wealth and money are joint with hers, so lest they would be given to a stranger, I married her." My father the prophet said, "Did you not hear the words of the Holy Bible, 'For what profit is it to a man if he gains the whole world, and loses his own soul? Or what will a man give in exchange for his soul?"

The man then said, "O my father, do I have any chance for repentance?" My father answered, "Yes you have." He took 150 dinar from his pocket and gave them to my father asking him to distribute them as charity. But my father answered, "This is not a place to take it is a place where we give. We are giving the poor and needy all the time. Arise and go to the cell of Abba Aflouh and you will find someone who will take that amount."

He left my father and headed to the monastery where he found Abba Paul so he gave him the gold. He took it happily and said, "You have done a favour to the brethren." He then had his blessing and left.

Arriving at his house he said to his wife, "You should know my sister that ignorantly we were living in sin." He narrated all what St. Shenouda the prophet had told him then left all the money to his wife and returned to his father St. Shenouda. He became a monk living a good life, struggling with patience till the end of his life.

Those Who Kill By the Sword
Will Die By the Sword

It happened one day that a man who lived in the village in Upper Egypt called Samhoud, in the region of the city of Epsoi came to my father the prophet St. Shenouda. He came in very great anguish of heart and he therefore sent a message into my father saying "O my holy father, I want to receive your blessing. It may be that be your holy prayers the mercy of God will come upon me so that God would forgive me my many sins for they are very many." St. Shenouda was informed of all that the man had said. My father said to the one who brought the message "Go and say to the man who has come, if you will obey me in what I shall say to you, you will see me. If you will not obey me, you will not look upon my face." The man said "I will obey you and do whatever you command."

When he entered, he knelt before my father in great humility. St. Shenouda said to him, "Confess your sins before us all so that you may be comforted from this great calamity." The man said, "My father, while I was sitting in my village, a man passed by me riding his colt with a purse hanging around his neck. I took my sword out of my pocket, ran after him and killed him. I then took the purse thinking that I would find a great quantity of gold which I would take and use to enjoy myself for many days. In it I found only 3 dinar. I then dug a hole in the ground, buried the man, then came straight to you. Now my father, what can I do that the Lord may forgive my great sin and have mercy on me?"

My father said to him, "Do not stay here. Arise now, go the city of Akhmim where you will find the prince. He has come south down the river and is being greeted by his people. Some thieves who robbed an eminent man will be brought to him. So you too must go and join the thieves and they will say that you are one of them. If the Prince asks you do not deny it. Thus he will kill you with them so the words are fulfilled, 'a soul for a soul' and you will enter the eternal life of God." The man left immediately and did exactly what my father had told him. The Prince killed him along with the other thieves. In this way the mercy of God came upon him just as my father told us.

Travelling By A Cloud

It happened on one occasion that the holy Patriarch Abba Kyrillos sent for my father St. Shenouda and Abba Victor the Archimandrite of Tabaneese on account of the impious Nestorius to withstand him. After they had entered the royal city, our righteous father St. Shenouda was walking into the king's palace when he found a grain of wheat which had been thrown away. He picked it up and put it in the pouch inside his cloak which was made of goatskin until he returned to his monastery. When the king had dismissed them so that they could go back to their own places, my father St. Shenouda went to board the ship with our holy fathers Abba Kyrillos and Abba Victor. But because the sails men did not know him due to his rugged clothes they said to him "You are not to go on board with the Patriarch." My father said to them "If not, then the Lord's will be done." Then he and his disciple who had gone with him went a short distance away and stood in prayer saying "O my Lord Jesus Christ. You took me out of my monastery and supported me in the King's palace and disgraced Nestorius the heretic. I am in need of Your mercy since the sails men have dismissed me and I have become a stranger and an outcast. Now my Lord Jesus Christ how will you take me to my monastery?"

While he was thinking these things to himself, behold a luminous cloud came down from heaven, lifted up both him and his disciple, snatched him up into the heights and flew off with him. When they reached the open sea, Abba Kyrillos looked up and saw my father St. Shenouda with his disciple in the middle of the cloud. They cried out saying "Bless us our holy father, the new Elijah." St. Shenouda said to him "Remember me O my holy father." In this way the cloud flew off with him and brought him to his monastery on the same day.

Now it was summertime there and the brothers were baking bread. He took the grain of wheat he had brought with him on his return from the King's palace and threw it under the millstone. The Lord sent so great an abundance of flour from the millstone that they were quite unable to gather it all up in bags. For three days and three nights this continued until they were exhausted and unable to gather and so they complained. So St. Shenouda went to the millstone, laid his palm branch upon it and said "Millstone I say to you cease." And it ceased immediately in accordance with the word of my father the righteous St. Shenouda, truly the man of God whose works are as powerful as those of the first prophets the apostles. Innumerable are his good deeds and the miracle which he accomplished by the grace of the Holy Spirit which was ever in him.

When the Patriarch Abba Kyrillos had arrived to his city in Alexandria, he sent for St. Shenouda and asked him "When

you were sitting on the cloud, how many days did it take
you to reach your monastery?" My father St. Shenouda said
to the Patriarch "Forgive me my holy father, I am unworthy
of such a thing." Abba Kyrillos said to him "I adjure you
by the prayers of the saints that you tell me what happened
to you and do not hide anything." My father said to him
humbly "Since you adjure me – I arrived to the monastery
on the very day on which we talked together, you from the
ship and I on the cloud. On the evening of the same day
I was at worship with the other brothers." The Patriarch
Abba Kyrillos and Abba Victor the Archimandrite were
immediately astonished and they therefore glorified God
who alone works miracles in His saints who do His will
and put their trust in Him. After this our holy father St.
Shenouda left them and returned to his monastery joyfully
reciting the words "Rejoice in the Lord, O you righteous!
For praise from the upright is beautiful."

Desiring To See A Ship

One day our father St Shenouda was sitting by a rock in the mountain's cave and with Him was our Lord Jesus Christ and they were talking together. Then my father the prophet said to him "My Lord, I would love to see a ship sailing here in the valley and wilderness." The Lord said to him "Tomorrow you will be given what you have desired" and He parted from him. A short time thereafter by the command of God the creator the place was filled with water and God caused a ship to come sailing by on the deep water which was there. The Lord Himself took the form of a captain and some angels took the form of the other sailors. The ship sailed on until it came to where the holy St. Shenouda was standing in prayer and the Lord said to him "Take the rope Shenouda and tie the ship." So he took the rope but could not find anything to tie it to. Then he went over to the hanging outcrop of rock and grasped it with his finger and thumb. At that very moment, it was immediately pierced through just like wax in front of a flame. He ran the rope through the stone and tied it and that stone is pierced to this very day as an everlasting sign for all generations. Full of joy our father St. Shenouda was reciting the psalm "What shall I render to the Lord for all His benefits towards me?"

The Devil Is Shamed

One day while my father was praying in a cave in the mountain east to his cell, suddenly the devil stood before him saying, "After all this struggle and toil are you not sure if the Nile will rise this year or not?" My father answered, "The will of God is controlling all things." So the devil said, "I also know this fact, and I am sure it will not rise this year." The righteous answered him, "You are a liar since the beginning. If it rises up I will not believe or trust you and if it does not I do not count on you at all." The devil said, "I will show you a miracle so that you might believe me (he was standing on a rock while my father was on another one praying towards the east); I will split this rock from the middle into two equal parts so that you would believe what I say." The devil turned to split the rock but the Lord did not want him to reach his aim therefore a small portion from the edge was split from the rock. My father said, "In the name of the Lord who broke the bread at that time, this rock will be split into two equal pieces" and so it happened. Thus the enemy fled in shame and this rock is still a witness to this miracle to which many people come and have its blessing in the name of my father St. Shenouda.

There is also a lake of water that never dries up, but is full of water at all times during all the days of the year. In winter, my father used to come and spend the day from evening till morning. Every night he would enter with his hands stretched like the Cross, praying all night. When it was sunrise, he would pray and go out to the valley next to Athribis from the north side walking towards his cell lest someone would see him. He used to lay down on the ground because of exhaustion till the sixth hour of the day, very tired from severe cold and vigil. He could not even crouch his legs or stretch them. Many times he blessed this valley which no one passed by. He would then go to his cell in peace, successful in his strife.

The Vision Of Hades

Our father St. Sthenouda was a prophet leading 2,200 monks and 1,800 nuns, excluding the juniors and those caring for them. He cared for and prayed on their behalf lest one soul should perish. Once at midnight, the angel of the Lord came and held his right hand and took him to show him the different punishments and their places. Going there, he saw virgins being tortured so he asked, "What did they do? What is this horrible fire which is never put out?" So they informed him that they were virgins in the body, but their tongues were sharp swords double-edged going everywhere talking about people and murmuring; this was why they were tortured because of their tongues. Examine yourself, o people, if you are indeed a pure virgin with your body, do not let your tongue go astray from God.

I, Shenouda, am telling you that I saw people being tortured in fire whom I knew as Christians. When they saw me they wept bitterly saying, "Intercede for us, our father Shenouda, that the Lord may give us a break, we are in severe torture. Plead for us that the Lord may cool our tongues with cold water". While I was praying on their behalf, our Lord Christ came and an angel came who was holding my hand and said, "Peace be to you. Have you seen these Shenouda? Many a time they have deformed My Image, so they deserve this punishment. Indeed if someone were to make handwork and others belittled his work or reproached him saying it was not a good one, would not the maker be angry with them as he they have defamed him? This is the case with the tongues of those who scorn the people whom My Hands have created. Oh the punishment that is reserved for those who murmur against others."

Our Saviour said to our righteous father, "You have to teach your monks, nuns and all your people not to do so to avoid this cursed pain." Then the righteous said, "My Master, I would like my children to visit Jerusalem to worship Your Holy Cross and Your footprints to be purified." So the Lord said to him, "You will be glorified in your monastery in Jerusalem which you have consecrated in My Name. Those who hear and do are equal to the angels. It is written that when a person left from Jericho to Jerusalem, the robbers attacked him. You have to know that My Cross is everywhere to whomever wants to repent and desires Me. He has to protect himself and he will be saved. Go in peace."

During summer, the ground was so hot under my fathers' feet, and because of his many tears, mud would be formed under his feet. He would form it in the shape of a brick and would stand over it. While praying and asking the Lord for the salvation of the human race, the brick would dissolve, becoming dust under his feet because of his abundant tears falling on it.

Visit To Heaven

It happened that St. Shenouda and Abba Victor were taken to the Heavenly Jerusalem to the assembly of the saints. They prayed and bowed to the Lord and they were told to sit down. A luminous angel in the shape of a monk came with a book in his hand, then for a long time he read the Revelation of St. John the Beloved of the Lord, then he farewelled them in peace and they went back to their dwelling places at this night in great joy.

A few days later, the Archimandrite from Tabanessi (Abba Victor) came to visit us and we met him with great joy. We talked about the wonders of God and my father said to him, "Do you remember the place which we went to, how beautiful and wonderful it was?" The elder Abba Victor answered, "Truly we rejoiced because of the brother who was reading in a sweet voice full of chastity." Our father –wanting to seem as though he did not know- answered, "What was he reading?" Abba Victor said, "He was reading the Apocalypses. I asked him if he reads it every day but he said only on Saturdays. Thus we ought to do the same in glorification to the Apocalypses of St. John. This was mentioned by the saintly fathers to glorify God."

Digging of The Well

One time our father St. Shenouda ordered that we should dig a well for the needs of the brethren. He delegated me for this, saying "Dig here in this place." I noticed that this place was shallow and so sought a higher place nearby and started digging. While the brothers were working there, the devil laid a trap for them. By his will, the well fell in on the labourers who were working there. When I knew it, I discovered my mistake and ran to my father since I know how merciful he is. When I saw him I fell on my knees kissing his feet. He said to me "Did I not show you the correct spot? Peace be with you and do not be afraid. Let the enemies of the Lord be disgraced." He arose, took his palm branch and drove it into the wall of the well saying "He who made the rod of Aaron to blossom, bless also this palm". It immediately took root and sent up palm branches and palm leaves. The men who were working ate its fruit. From that day to this, the well has never moved again.

Christ Speaks Concerning
The End Times

It happened one day that our Saviour was sitting and talking with my father St. Shenouda. I, Wissa his disciple came in wanting to meet Him but He immediately withdrew. After I had come in and received the blessings from my father, I asked him "My holy father. Who was that talking with you? Where did He go when I came in?" My father the prophet sad to me "It was the Lord Jesus Christ who was with me just now, speaking mysteries to me." I said to him "I too would like to see Him so that He might bless me." My father said to me "You will not be able to see him because you are only a novice." I said to him "I am a sinner my holy father." He said to me "It is not so but you are faint-hearted." Again in tears I said to him "I beg you my father, let your mercy come upon me so that I too may be worthy to see Him." My father said to me "If you wait until the 6th hour tomorrow, come in then. You will find me sitting down with Him. See that you say nothing at all."

On the following day, I came in accordance with my father's instructions and as was the custom, knocked on the door so that I might go in and receive a blessing. Straight away the Lord departed from Him. I wept bitterly and said "I am wholly unworthy to see the Lord in the flesh." But my father said to me "He will comfort your heart, Wissa my son, and let you hear His sweet voice. So then at one time, though it was more than I deserve, I heard Him speaking with my father and I have been grateful to Him all the days of my life.

I heard Him many times talking to my father. One day, my father came out with a sad countenance so I asked him, "What happened today my father to have such a sad face?" He answered, "We have to weep for ourselves and for everyone else. Truly it is good if some are not born into the world, because our Lord Jesus Christ has informed me on this day about tribulations and sufferings telling me, "Tell your children and write them so that they awaken and are chastised. All of them should be cautious lest they should slip and yield their souls to the devil."

I said to him, "My holy father, tell us about these tribulations and sufferings and pray that we might also not fall in them." My father said, "My children, I am announcing to you what Christ has shown me will happen at the end of the ages. When I left you and entered into my cell in the wilderness, while I was reciting my prayers in the cave under the mountain, the Lord came and said to me 'Peace be to you Shenouda', so I answered, 'Welcome O Great Lord, the Lord of heaven and earth.' The devil then appeared in the form of a worker carrying a bag of new hay. He stopped and scattered it on us towards the south in disrespect. As for me, I stood up, held his head and hit him with a rock, but the Lord said to me, "Refrain Shenouda, his time is not due yet', so I left him ashamed in a great scandal.

Then I told the Saviour, "Why is he also against us always?" So the Saviour answered, "Me and My Father have kept him since the beginning of the world to distinguish our chosen that resist him. I will tell you about what will happen before it happens; the Persians will rise against the people in Mousal in great strength, then they will come to Egypt. There will be a great massacre, loitering the money of the Egyptians, selling their children with gold because of the extreme persecution and cruelty of the Persians. Many masters will become slaves, and many slaves will become masters. Woe to Egypt because of the Persians for they will take the church utensils and drink wine in them before the altar with no fear or remorse. They will also rape the women before their husbands. There will be great tribulation and ordeals.

One third of those who will survive will die because of sadness and depression. Then after a little while, the Persians will depart Egypt and the Antichrist will come to the Romans and will appoint two leaders from the princes and the bishops. He will then enter Egypt, occupy it, and perform many wonders. He will build trenches and fortresses, and will order to build the gates of the cities in the wilderness and the deserts. He will destroy the east and the west and then chase the Patriarch, the one who is caring for the Christians living in Egypt. He will dismiss him and then the Patriarch will come to the place near Timan. The Patriarch will then come saddened to your Monastery.

Reaching this place, I will restore him to his seat once more.

Then the children of Ishmael and the children of Esau will persecute the rest of the Christians. The rest of them will decide to rule and own the entire earth. They will as well begin the building of the Temple of Jerusalem. Know when this happens that the end of the ages is near and that the Jews are waiting for the Antichrist, preceding the other nations at his arrival. If you see the abomination of desolation mentioned by Daniel the Prophet in the holy place, and those who deny My sufferings which I tolerated on the Cross while they are inside my church. Truly they do not fear or care for anything.

Those who crucify me agree with the Antichrist and reject my Holy Resurrection. Let the reader understand, because he is ready to delude the rest of the vain world, trying to mislead my chosen ones, but they will not follow him as I will save them from his hands. Those who will follow him he will mark them on their foreheads and right hand. Then this demoralized one will prevent anyone without his mark to sell or buy. He will proudly heal the sick claiming he is Christ. Thus they will praise him saying, "If you are the Christ ask this rock to be moved and be dropped in the sea" so the rock will move in front of the eyes of the atheists but not the believers.

Then there will be great inflation, so all those who believe in him will come saying, "Give us bread to eat lest we should perish out of hunger." He will give them a lot of gold, but they will contend with him saying, "Shall we eat gold and be nourished?" Then they will throw their gold and silver in the streets and cry for the loss of them. They will come back to him saying, "If you are the Christ give us water to drink" but he will become so angry with them and persecute them with great tribulations.

Woe to the pregnant and nursing women in these days, they will cut the bellies of the pregnant. He will take the poison off the teeth of the dragons and put it in the weapons and fighting equipment's. Woe to those who listen to him and obey his words. My chosen ones whom I love know this fact, they will flee to the deserts and wilderness where I have prepared for them, then they will begin to say to the mountains, "Fall on us!" and to the hills, "Cover us". They will plead to me and I will have mercy on them. I will provide them with fruits to grow in the valleys, and water out of the springs and wells.

My chosen Shenouda, I am Christ speaking with you. Warn them when people say Christ is here or there, do not believe them for this will be the Antichrist, for as the lightning comes from the east and flashes to the west, so also will the coming of the Son of Man be, thus be cautious and remember what I have said to you. Men will go and dig at the bottom of the sea for water but will not find any. They will only find mud which they will use to cool themselves with.

The Antichrist will take their children and squeeze them under the stones of squeeze. The wild animals will come out of the holes and caves and devour the disobedient ones. They will suffer the bites -which are like those of a scorpion-

for six months. People will suffer great tribulations and injustice from the rulers who will loot their children and their treasures. People will hate and yield each other to death. Strong injustice will be on the earth as a result of the sins of the people on the earth. They will deceive each other, there will be no more good deeds; no one will love justice, starting from the leaders to the subordinates. The rulers of these days will unjustly collect a lot of money; they will forget all about pleadings and prayers and reject my church for they will live in immortality. This will all happen during this generation because of the evil which dominates them, their many sins and iniquities. This nation is the sceptre of my wrath and the power of my discontent.

Woe to the leaders and the heads of the nations in all the cities, villages and monasteries. They will suffer greatly from those who rule over them because of money. I have announced to you, my chosen Shenouda, the signs of the end. In addition, when the Antichrist who aggravates the whole creation appears, I will send my prophets Enoch and Elijah while he is still dominant and committing these iniquities. They will expose him that he is not the Christ, but rather the deceiver of all the nations. The Antichrist will be enraged, he will kill them and leave their corpses in the streets of Jerusalem for three days, then I will give them the breath of life and they will resist him. They will warn the rest of the nations about the eternal life to come, and that they will have rest during the 1000 years banquet and its goodness which I have prepared for my chosen ones who believe in the Holy Trinity. This is the first Resurrection. Then comes the second Resurrection, the dead will come back without decay, those who were killed by the swords, or devoured by the lions, or were burnt or drowned.... all the dead by various means will come back.

This is My will, I am the Lord talking to you will resurrect them in My Second Resurrection. They will be gathered together in the valley of Jehoshaphat. I will reward each one according to his deeds. You and the apostles will sit and judge justly those who did good deeds to the Resurrection of Life and those who did evil to the Resurrection of condemnation. Now I have told you my chosen Shenouda and made you a prophet till the end. There is none likened to you to whom I have revealed what I have said, so that you might pass it to your children and all the people to keep it and live with Me in My Paradise.

Peace be with you, Shenouda, the beloved of My Father. Reveal to them what I have revealed to you."

Then He ascended to the heavens while His angels were praising Him. I have now told you and the Christian brethren all what the Lord has disclosed unto me. Let us strife and be cautious not to sin. The Lord is kind and merciful, He forgives our sins so that we avoid the indignation on the Day of Judgment and the death of those who reject and deny the Lord, those who will inherit destruction on that day. Oh! What a fearful Day, the Day of despair and regret, the Day of sigh and sadness, the Day of severe hardship. Woe to all the sinners on that frightening Day because the Lord has said with His pure mouth that the dead will resurrect without decay, but He will mark the bodies of the sinners with a black mark, and their rotten sins will be a stench.

As for the righteous, their faces will shine as the sun in the Paradise of their Father, and their sweet aroma will spread everywhere because of their good deeds, the angels will rejoice and clothe them in glorified attires.

Our King will judge in justice and fairness. There is no partiality between young or old, priest or slave, sinner or righteous but He gives each one according to his deeds. Oh that last verdict falling on the sinners condemning them to Hell! What a statement that shall never be changed! What a wail that will never be comforted because those who go to Hades on that day will not be visited by anyone forever.

Also listen to the verdict full of happiness and joy as He says to the righteous, "Enter into the joy of your Lord." Blessed are those who deserve to hear the voice full of joy. The heavens will be folded as a cloth and the earth will vanish away. There will be a new earth and a new heaven according to the orders of the Lord, where the righteous and pious dwell forever. They will not be given to marriage but will be like angels of God; as the Lord has revealed to those who say there is no resurrection.

Now my children, let us do our best and weep for our sins before they visit us. We are not living here forever. You must know that your life is short on earth, what is the benefit of this world? Only sorrow, sadness, pain and suffering, void deeds, an adornment without fruits. O wretched man, have they fixed an age for you on earth and informed you about it? Have they told you that you will never die? Do you want to live on earth 969 years as Methuselah? When the Lord cursed the sinners since the beginning He said: "My Spirit shall not strive with man forever, for he is indeed flesh; yet his days shall be one hundred and twenty years," if longer, it will be all toil and hardships.

My beloved children; you must know that man will not live forever in this world, we are losing people every day but we are not warned. Indeed where is your father and grandfather? Will you last forever? You might say I am still young and have not reached my father's age when he died; indeed I am telling you that younger people than yourself die every day, your son might die before you enjoy his presence in your bosom. The same with a groom taken from his bride, a son from his brother before being satisfied from looking at him.

Woe to us, for this one day will certainly reach us all. Let us be ready before they come to take us. Let us light our lamps at all times so that when the Bridegroom comes He might find us ready and we can enter with Him into the eternal wedding. Beware to be likened to the foolish virgins who slumbered and slept, whose lams were going out. What are these lamps, which the Saviour spoke about? I will tell you: we will resemble them to the souls of the human beings, the oil to the prayers, vigils, fasting, love, patience, love of the neighbour, love of God and His holy church and all of the good virtues, for these are the fruits of life if they depart the body to inherit with Christ the everlasting goodness.

These are the permanent characteristics of the sinners who died while in their slumber in evil thoughts: lying, envy, anger, stealing, murmur, hatred, ignorance, insulting parents, deceiving, enmity, homosexuality, licentiousness, pride, stubbornness, denying of faith, haughtiness, excessive talking in the church during prayers and hymns while the Body and Blood of our Lord Jesus Christ is present on the holy altar. About these, it was said that the words of Christ became like sneer and rebuke, they never loved Him. These will not enter with the Bridegroom into His Paradise. Truly, if the master of the house had known what hour the thief would come, he would have watched, and not have allowed his house to be broken into.

Now my brethren, let us awaken from our negligence and slumber waiting for the coming of our Lord Jesus Christ, so that whenever He comes to release us from this body He would find us without sin before Him and grant us the eternal goodness."

This is was what our father St. Shenouda told and instructed us to do for our sake. We have informed you with everything for the glory of God and His saint, St. Shenouda. May his blessings be with us all. Amen.

Now we will go back to the miracles performed by God through him.

The Blessing of The Bakery

It happened once that there was a great drought and the inhabitants of the region of Akhmim and those of the region of Ebsay came in a crowd to my father to be fed by him. My father gave them bread until the loaves ran out. The brother who was in charge of baking the bread came to my father St. Shenouda and said "That was a great deal of bread my father. How will you now feed the multitudes who have gathered to us and the monks? In reply, my father said to me and to the one who distributed the loaves "Go and gather all the left over loaves together with all the little fragments and crumbs. Moisten them and give them to the crowds to eat."

We then went off in accordance with his word and gathered them up. We left nothing behind. We went back to him and told him "we have left nothing behind". He said to us "Pray to God that He will bring about such a blessing that you can feed them all." We obeyed him and when the time came, we went to open the bread store and the abundance of God poured forth upon us while we were still outside the door of the bread store. We have called it since 'the treasure of blessing'. In this way the multitudes ate and when they were full they glorified God.

It happened once that the bakers complained about the ashes they had to carry away from cleaning the furnace. Our father St. Shenouda knew this and said to them "How many ovens are there?" They said to him "There are eleven." My father said to them "Go and throw all the ashes which you normally bring from the ten ovens into the one in the middle. I trust in God and the prayers of the saints that it will never be filled up." This they did in accordance with his true word, all the ashes which they brought from the ten ovens, they packed into the one in the middle. From that day until now it has not filled up.

Building of The Church

Before they had yet built the church, our Lord Jesus appeared to our father St. Shenouda and said "Arise, measure out the church and the foundation of the monastery and build a sanctuary in My name and yours. It will be called 'The Holy Congregation, for saints will gather in it and people from all nations will seek to look at it." My father St. Shenouda said to the Lord "My Lord, where shall I find anything to spend on the building of a sanctuary." The Lord said to him "Arise and go to your dwelling place in the desert. Pick up what you will find on the way and spend it on the sanctuary. You may perhaps think that this is the Devils doing, it is not. It is instead the means whereby you build the church and the monastery in accordance with My will. I the Lord have spoken."

Our father, for his part, then arose and went into the inner desert and spent the whole night there in prayer. When he had left and was on his way out in the morning, he found a small leather bag of gold so he stretched out his hand, picked it up and went to the monastery. Then and there our Lord Jesus Christ came to our father and they went off together and laid out the foundation of the sanctuary. It happened that one of the stones were not used because it was not suitable for building. I left it to the will of the Lord and with this stone, our Lord and my father laid the foundation of the church. My father then arranged for the works man and craftsmen, the stone masons and the carpenters – they worked on the church and with the Lord helping them in all that they did, with everything they needed, they completed it in six months.

The chief of the builders had received his full wages. He also made a nice crown and hanged it on top of the altar's dome in glorification to our Lord and in honouring our father the saint, and as a benefit for himself. His work and commemoration is still there in the sanctuary of the saints. His brother noticed what he did, so he also made a cross ornamented with gold and silver and hanged it in the middle of the ceiling of the church. Thus what is written was fulfilled, "I will take all what I have and make it a crown in honouring my Master and for the glory of His saints forever". Amen.

A Man Tests St. Shenouda

It happened once that a man came to our father St. Shenouda. He was a man from Bahnasa and he had with him 20 dinars. Someone else, a friend of his, came with him and the man said to his friend "I want to give a small gift to the sanctuary of St. Shenouda, to be given as alms for my salvation. However I am not going to hand them over until I know first whether the great man will give them as alms or not." So he gave the 20 denarius to the friend who had come with him, dressed himself in worn clothes and entered the monastery. He went to my father the prophet, St. Shenouda, and spoke to him saying "I beg you my holy father have mercy upon me and give me a small gift of just 20 denarius so that I can give them to the moneylender, otherwise he will throw me out of my house and take it from me." My father said to him "This is not a time my son for testing. Perhaps you would like another 20 denarius to add to the 20 denarius which you brought when you came because you would like to accumulate a great amount. Truly you must give an account for your actions." Then St. Shenouda called a fellow monk and said to him, "Go along a certain road to the field. You will find a man sitting on the ground, combing his hair and having a pitcher of water in his hand. Say to him 'your friend says 'just as I said to you, sit here until I find out whether the great man will give them as charity or not. I say to you arise and come to me."

When the monk had gone off to the field as my father had commanded him, he found the man and said to him the words which my father had told him. The man who had come to my father was standing by him in great astonishment. Then he exclaimed "Truly I know today that there is a prophet in this monastery, just as I have seen it with my own eyes." After this, he gave the money to my father St. Shenouda. After they had prayed, the two of them departed from him in peace, glorifying God in his saints.

The Man From The Foreign Country

One day there was a man from a distant foreign country. When he had heard of the miracles of our righteous father St. Shenouda, he came to receive a blessing from him. My father replied to him, "How shall I bless you when you have committed a great and most grievous sin." The man replied to my father saying, "I do not know what sin I have committed. I am a Christian and I have believed in the God of heaven since I was a child." My father said to him, "Do you not remember the day when you ate, drank and slept in your house and while you were sleeping, the enemy the devil deceived you. You arose, took your sword, went out and found a woman and slit open her belly with your sword." The man replied, "Truly my holy father, what you say is true. Yet if a sinful man does penance does he not receive forgiveness?" My father said to him "There is indeed repentance. If you endure the chastisement I shall give you, God will forgive you. For God does not wish the death of a sinner but that he leaves his evil path and repents. Do good and live." As soon as the man heard these words of our father, he cut his hair and put on the monastic clothes, struggling gloriously until the day of his death.

The third day after he had been made a monk, he filled a pitcher with water and my father went with him into the inner desert until he was 13 miles from the monastery. There he left him in a cave. The cave was circular just as large as he was tall. The door of the cave opened out above him like a window. My father St. Shenouda used to visit him once a week in order to see him and bless him on Saturday, on the Lord's Day and bring him what he needed for the week, a small pitcher of water and a small loaf of bread.

A year after he had been made a monk, my father went in to him and said, "What has happened to you? Tell me." The man replied, "Just when the night had given way to first light, I saw my body shaking so badly that I said 'All my sinews have been pulled from my body' and I was troubled, thinking that I would soon die. After this, behold an object which stank dreadfully like a rotten corpse came out of my body. It went down a cleft in the rock like a smoky vapour, floated away and disappeared. I myself was in a stupor until you called inside to me." The holy St. Shenouda replied, "Be comforted. Today salvation has come upon you and the Lord has forgiven your sin. After this, my father took him and brought him back to the monastery among the brethren. Then I, Wissa the disciple of the holy old man, went to my father and said, "Is this not the man from a foreign country who once came to us?" He said to me, "It is." I said to him, "Where has he been all this time." My father replied, "After an evil beast had wounded him, I took him to the doctor. He healed him and salvation came upon him." The brother glorified God all his days.

The Help Of Those
Who Seek His Refuge

One day a man from the town of Akhmim came to him. He was a notable businessman of very great wealth. Thieves had robbed his house leaving him nothing. He came to my father and cried, "Help me my Lord and father, they have devastated my house and left me nothing at all." My father St. Shenouda replied, "Arise, go north to the town of Assiut. You will find three men sitting on the ground outside the door of the city gate. One of them will be combing his hair, say to him 'Shenouda says come to me so that I may speak with you about a certain matter' and the man will talk with you." So after he had received blessing, the businessman departed and went north to the town of Assiut. He found the three men sitting on the ground outside the city gate, just as my father had told him, and one of them was combing his hair. To him the businessman said, "Friend, the man of God St. Shenouda says 'come to me so that I may speak with you and tell you of this matter.'" The man said to him, "Indeed, behold for many years I have wanted to see that holy man to receive a blessing from him." There and then the two of them arose and set off together and came to the holy St. Shenouda and received his blessing. He said to them, "Sit down for a little while and rest." After this, my father spoke with the man he had sent for, he who had robbed the business man's house, and said to him, "My son, go and give back to the man the possessions which you have stolen and carried away. I will make him give you a few of them." The man was afraid and said to my father, "It was not I alone who carried them off." My father said to him, "I know that too my son." The man said to my father, "If he will not tell anyone at all, I will take him and give back his possessions complete and intact." Then my father called the businessman and made him take an oath saying, "I will never reveal the matter to the day of my death." So he took him and gave him back all his possessions as they were, just as our father St. Shenouda had commanded and the businessman gave him a small portion of his possessions and sent him away.

Afterwards, the businessman came back again to our father the prophet and received his blessing. My father St. Shenouda said to him, "Look my son, you want to go the city of Alexandria. Do me this favour, after you arrive, buy the first thing you come across for sale and bring it to me. Whatever you give for it I will give to you, when by God's will, you return to me." On his way to Alexandria, as soon as he disembarked from the ship, he found a man who had a silver tray used for the altar which the man had stolen and carried off from one of the monasteries of our father St. Shenouda. When the businessman saw the silver tray with the name of St. Shenouda written on it he said to himself, "If I buy this silver tray and take it to the great man of God, I will be ashamed to take anything from him for he had pity on me, told me about my possessions and had them given back to me. I will not buy it lest I lose something else with my own hands." When he had went in to the city of Alexandria and again met the man with the tray, he did not buy it. After another two days, he once more met the man carrying the tray in everyone's presence and again he did not buy it. When the businessman had sold his goods and went down to the river to board the ship, the man came again with the tray and again he did not buy it. One of the sailors on the ship, which the businessman had boarded, bought it for 4 denarius and he said to himself, "I will take it to the sanctuary of St. Shenouda the man of God." When they arrived at their city, the sailor took the tray, brought it to the monastery offering it to St. Shenouda saying, "Would you like to buy this silver tray?" My father said to him, "Indeed I would like to buy it. But tell me how much you paid for it my son?" The sailor replied, "8 denarius." St. Shenouda said to him, "No my son, see that you do not lie. It was instead 4 denarius that you paid for it." The sailor said to him, "Truly you are a saint." St. Shenouda said to him, "My son take 5 denarius for it" but the sailor said to him, "I will take nothing for it. Remember me in your prayers." So after receiving his blessings, he left St. Shenouda glorifying God and St. Shenouda said to him "may the Lord reward you double fold."

After a month had passed, the same businessman to whom St. Shenouda had caused the restoration of his possessions, the same businessman who was instructed to buy the first thing for sale on his journey, came to visit the monastery. He came and said to my father, "While I was out walking I dropped a bag of gold and I do not know where it fell." Now it happened that it was the sailor who found this bag of gold which had been dropped and it contained 60 denarius but the businessman did not know this and he entreated my father to have mercy on him but my father said to him, "This is destiny. The riches of this world are like a prostitute. She is in your house today but tomorrow she makes a contract with someone else. Now my son, God has given the gold you lost to whom He wills and you shall never find it." Thus the businessman left in anguish of heart and in great shame.

There was one time some people came to my father very dismayed with tattered clothing. They knelt for a long while before him then said, "Have mercy upon us! All our possessions were stolen and we have nothing left as you can see. We were advised to keep hold of our neighbours and those who live in our street, and now we came to you our father." They spent the night and the next morning my father said to their eldest, "Take your son, go back to your house and after three days come to me alone." This man was hard-hearted who never had mercy on people. After three days when he came back, my father said to him, "Be kind and merciful to the poor, give them alms generously for our Lord Jesus Christ has said give and you will receive."

The man was so frightened of him and said, "I swear with the name of the Lord and through your prayers if I get my money back I will give a big amount of it to the poor and the needy." My father said, "Go to this very distant cell from us towards the north and sit next to the hut there. Then three men who live in this city will pass by you, one of them will say "Let us sit here and have some lunch." The other two will say, "no way." Then they will sit with you for a little while. When they decide to leave, go quickly with them, hold the one on your left and tell him, "Our father Shenouda wants you", so he will come with you.

The man did as ordered by our father, he came with the man to my father. He kissed his hand saying, I have had a great blessing today when I saw you." My father answered, "My son, do mercy to me for the sake of God and give this man his utensils and textiles lest the Lord your God would take everything from you. You have surpassed your limits!"

The man then said. "You know my father that I did not steal them alone." My father answered, I only asked for you because I know you would never disobey me. Your friends are hard-hearted and stubborn, they will perish if they do not listen to me." The man said to my father, "Let us go to the altar so that this man might swear with the name of God not to tell anyone about this matter. If he gives me a little money, I will give him back all his textiles untouched." They did as he had said, then they took the man to a secret place and gave him back all his possessions. The man thus gave many alms and gifts to the poor as instructed by my father.

This was the story our father informed us about so that all the people may hear and glorify God.

The Faithful Youth

There was a pious God-fearing youth from the city of Akhmim who used to come frequently to the Monastery. He was married in chastity and always did his best to come to us every Saturday and Sunday. A woman went on board the ferry with him. It happened that a strong storm whirled and the woman became slightly uncovered because of the strong wind. When he saw her, he desired her in his heart. He was at that time carrying the Orban (holy bread) with him. When the ferry had arrived everyone had departed. He went back to his wife and was calmed down. He then came back with his servant carrying the Orban. He sat alone and ordered his servant to take the Orban to my father but as for my father, he knew what had happened. The next morning, the man came to my father very ashamed of himself. My father smiled and said, "Why did you not have Communion yesterday my son?" The man answered, "Truly my father the Spirit of God dwelling in you has informed you what has happened to me." So he comforted him quietly saying, "Blessed are you my son. You will have all good things because you have followed the paths of the kings, travelling through the narrow way and fulfilled your desire from the allowed source. The Lord has accepted your offering."

Then my father gave Communion to the youth and the congregation with his holy hands, then he went back to his house glorifying God.

Theodosius Requests A Visit

Great signs and many miracles were worked by the hands of my holy father St. Shenouda. His fame spread even to the pious kings. They were told that there is man in the south (Upper Egypt) called Shenouda, whatever he says truly comes to pass. It happened one time that one of the pious kings wrote a letter to St. Shenouda saying, "I, Theodosius Junior and unworthy king, to whom God has given the kingdom despite my unworthiness, write to you O holy father Shenouda. I beseech you to hasten to visit us so that we may and all my citizens, be worthy of all your blessings. The entire kingdom is looking forward to your visit to us. Please do not hesitate to come to us, we thirst for you and your holy teachings according to the things which those who have come to us tell us about the gifts which God has performed through you. Remember us in your holy prayers. Farewell in the name of the Holy Trinity." He stamped the letter and gave it to his personal caretaker who was called Eudoxious who went to the governor of Ansena who then took him to my father to the monastery. After receiving his blessings they sat down and the caretaker brought out the letters of the king and presented them to St. Shenouda. When my father St. Shenouda received the letters he began to read and he reached the passage where it was written 'make haste to visit us'. He was then greatly grieved and deeply afflicted and said to the caretaker, "What does the king want with me? I am a poor and wretched man here in this monastery, praying and supplicating for my sins." The caretaker said to him, "They wish to enjoy your blessings." My father said to him, "Look, perhaps you may excuse me from this visit for I am an old man." He answered, "Do not hinder this visit for I cannot disobey the order of my king." So my father told me, I Wissa his son, to offer hospitality for the visitors and provide them rest from their journey until the Lords will be done.

After they had spent two days in the monastery, the caretaker entreated my father saying, "Arise and let us go lest the king be angry with us." My father St. Shenouda said to him, "Do me this favour and tell the king that the man is old and could not come." The caretaker said to him, "If you do not come willingly then there are soldiers here who will take you unwillingly." My father said to him, "If that is the case, grant me this day until tomorrow and if God wills, we shall go." When evening came my father entered the sanctuary and stretched out his hands in prayer asking for direction saying, "O Lord, you brought me out of my mother's womb. Hear me for I am in need of Your mercy and compassion." While he was still praying a bright cloud and two angels came from heaven saying, "Peace be with you O beloved of Christ. We will now take you to the king." Thus the words of the prophet Isaiah were fulfilled, "Then you shall call, and the Lord will answer; You shall cry, and

He will say, 'Here I am."

The cloud immediately snatched him up, flew away with him to the kings palace, in the place where the king was. There was a great luminous light where he was sleeping and so the king leaping in fear, fell to the ground saying, "Who are you in such a glory? For I am very disturbed." My father St. Shenouda said, "I am Shenouda the monk for whom you sent. By the order of the Lord Christ, rise up and do not be afraid. The peace of the Lord Jesus Christ will be with you in your era O son of the Orthodox kings. What do you want with me a sinner that you trouble your soldiers to fetch me, a feeble monk?" The king said to him, "How did you get here and how many days did you spend on the journey?" My father said to the king, "It was Christ Jesus the son of the living God and His angels who brought me here to you so that I may satisfy you fully in what you have determined. Before I came to you I was at worship this very evening with the brothers in the monastery." The king said to him, "Where is the caretaker and the soldiers I sent to you?" St. Shenouda replied and said to the king, "They are asleep in the monastery." The king in great faith said, "Truly before this day I had heard with my ears of your miracles but today I have seen them face to face. I have sent for you because I, together with the entire kingdom wait to enjoy your holy blessing and your blessed prayers. Pray for us that the Barbarians might not hurt or bother us."

My father raised his right hand and blessed the king saying, "May Jesus Christ bless you O king who loves God and all your city. May He establish your throne like that of your holy fathers Archadius and Onorius. May He submit all your enemies to you and humiliate them. May He perfect you all in the faith of your fathers, confirming and guarding the precepts and faith of our fathers the apostles. May you be worthy to hear His voice full of joy 'Well done, good and faithful servant. Enter into the joy of your Lord.'" He then signed the king with the sign of the cross three times and the king who had ailment in his body found that it was taken away. The king said to my holy father, "Stay with us a few days my holy father so that we may enjoy you to the full." My father said to him, "It is necessary for me to go. Do not delay those who brought me to you because they are under authority. Do me this favour and write a letter in your name which I may give to the caretaker so that he and those with him may return to you in peace and not trouble me in trying to bring me to you yet again." The king said to him, "Whatever you order me I will do it happily" and immediately he wrote this message: 'I Theodosius the king, write to you Eudoxious. As soon as you receive these letters from our holy father the prophet St. Shenouda, the priest, the monk, the archimandrite of the whole earth who in a way God alone knows, came to me this very night to the place where I sleep – make haste to return and do not try to bring him to me.' He also wrote to him on certain other secret matters which were just between the king and the caretaker and then sealed the letter with his ring and gave it to St. Shenouda who after he embraced and received his blessings, let him go.

Thereupon the cloud with the two angels again lifted up my father and took him to the monastery the same night and that same night, before the break of day, he was at worship with the brothers. No one knew that he had gone to the king and had returned to his monastery. When morning came, the caretaker came and said to my father, "Arise and let us go so that the king may not be angry with me." My father said to him, "Look my son, go to the king and tell him that I am an old man." The caretaker said to him, "If you do not come willingly, I will take you against your will." When my father had heard this, he put his hand in his garb and brought out the kings letter and handed it to him. When the caretaker saw it he recognised it as the king's and so looked in amazement at my father. My father signed him with the cross and said to him, "Open it and read it." When he began to read it and came upon the matters which were a secret between himself and the king, he threw himself down at my father's feet and said, "Truly my Lord and father, you are a man whose feet the world is not worthy since. I would like to say with you and become a monk for from now on I will not leave you." My father said to him, "No my son. Arise and go to the king instead, for he is asking for you and he loves and is in need of you." The caretaker said to him, "Do me this favour then and bless me before I leave O friend of God and a dwelling place of the Holy Spirit." So my father blessed him saying, "May the Lord Jesus Christ bless you and deliver you from the snares of the devil and may you inherit the good things which endure forever." So he left my father together with those who accompanied him, and the letter and went to the king glorifying God with great peace.

Who Is Like St. Anthony?

It happened one day that some of the men of the city of Akhmim came to St. Shenouda because they wanted to receive is blessings. With them came certain monks of great renown from Wadi El Natrun who wanted to hear his words. They said to him, "Will there be a monk in this generation like the blessed St. Anthony in his devoutness, virtues and worship?" My father said to them, "Even if all monks of this time and those to come after, came together in a single place, they would not make a single Anthony." They were amazed about the words of our father the prophet and so when they had received his blessings, they glorified God. They then asked him also, "We have been thinking for a long time about this matter and we want you to clarify it for us; people, cattle and birds are always drinking from this river. Would the water decrease or would it not? My father answered, "The earth is the Lord's -blessed be His Name - at all times. It is well known that everyone uses this river. They cannot live without drinking. The Lord is Marvellous and His miracles are numerous, at the time of the River Nile flood, the water will increase." They praised my father saying: "We are comforted by your words" then they left glorifying the Lord.

To Be With Christ
Rather Than People

One day our father and our Lord Jesus Christ were sitting down talking together. Just then, behold, the bishop of the city of Akhmim passed by the monastery. He wanted to go to Alexandria to see the Patriarch and on his way he wanted to visit my father. He sent in a request to my father saying, "Make haste to come to me so that I can meet you before I travel." Now at that time my father did not open the door to the servant as he was sitting with the saviour who was comforting him for his toil and worship. The servant went back to the bishop informing him that St. Shenouda was not free for him. The bishop answered according to his authority, "If he does not come and meet me, he will be considered disobedient and will be excommunicated." The servant returned to my father and said to him what the bishop had told him. My father replied, "Behold, here sitting with me is He who created heaven and earth. I will not go while I am with Him." Then the Saviour said to my father, "Arise and go to the bishop so that you may be absolved lest he excommunicate you, for behold he will die after three days. Otherwise I will not let you enter heaven because of the covenant that I made with Peter saying, 'What you bind on earth will be bound in heaven and what you loose on earth will be loosed in heaven." When my father heard these words of our Saviour, he arose immediately and rushed to meet the bishop and greeted him joyfully. The bishop then asked him, "Why were you hiding from me all this time in your monastery and would not come out to meet me?" The saint said to him in meekness, "Forgive me, my father. Believe me when you sent for me, with me was One sitting with me and He would not allow me to come to you until He departed when he wished to. Here I am coming to you to kiss your hands." The bishop consented to what he had said, and as if an angel woke him up he said to my father, "You are absolved now and forever Amen." Then he came back safely to us to the Monastery, the bishop headed to Assuit where he died exactly as our Lord Jesus Christ had told my father.

As for me, I said to my father, "The judgment of the Lord is upright. The Lord has decided that this man would not die while visiting us. Then my father informed us about what the Saviour had told him that he would die after three days. Then my father said to me, "When I came close to the bishop, I saw John the Celibate pointing to me with his right hand saying: "Follow him that he might absolve you."

Test of Partiality

I will tell you of this miracle: The angel of the Lord held my father's hand, took him and showed him a holy land. The angel asked him to build on that spot a church in the Name of the Holy Trinity, and he did as he was told. A few days later while he was in this church, the angel of the Lord held his hand and took him to his Monastery. My father changed his appearance and sat by the door steps like a stranger to test the passing by brethren. He said to some of them "Keep the law of the Lord and the rules established for you by your father." Some of them were upset with him. They went and informed the rest, then they came back to know who he was. They said to him, "Where are you from? We have seen many strangers coming to us but none of them have talked to us in such a manner."

When my father noticed their impoliteness in their hearts he disclosed to them that he was the abbot of the Monastery. They were greatly frightened and were about to die out of shame, some of them could not even move from their spot. Some fled, and some greeted him kissing his hands while saying: "Welcome back, O you the shepherd guiding his flock. We were so thirsty for you like a dry land waiting for irrigation. Forgive us our father and have mercy on our brethren, you know that the devil hates us, so be kind to them and to us."

My father was sympathetic. He lifted those who were bowing and comforted the rest, and they all rejoiced for his return, chanting and praising in reverence and great dignity before him. As for my father, because of his exceeding holiness, purity and sweet voice, he read the chapter in the Holy Bible which speaks of the seeds which fell on good ground yielded a crop: some a hundredfold, some sixty and some thirty. After addressing these useful words, they benefited much and their souls rejoiced for his return. May his prayers be with us. Amen.

Power Over The Devil

One day while my father was sitting in the monastery, the devil and a host of other demons with him, came and spoke to my father with great threats and violence and wickedness. When my father saw the devil he recognised him immediately and straight away sprang up upon him and grappled with him. He seized him, held him to the ground and placed his foot on his head saying, "Who do you think you are coming in such great dare?" He kept hitting him on the floor and the Lord granted him great strength so my father's right foot was upon the devil's chest, and he shouted at the rest of them to go behind him. The devil and his army said to my father: "Since the day you came to Abba Pigol at a young age, you are always dismissing us up till today." So he released them and they left in shame and disgrace.

A Spirit Bearer

It happened one day that Abba Mardarious was heading towards Constantinople to the king Theodosius. When he had arrived in the neighbourhood of the monastery he said, "Before we travel north, let us go to the prophet St. Shenouda and receive his blessings." A young monk called John replied hastily and proudly, "What prophet? Let us move on for indeed he does not even know what he ate yesterday." When they approached the monastery, my father went out to greet them and took them into the monastery. When they had prayed and sang hymns they sat down. Straight away my father the prophet spoke saying, "Where is the brother John? So they all looked at each other in wonder. Then he came and bowed down, so my father seized him saying, "Truly I do not know what I ate yesterday. Yet on the day of judgement, this withered body which is now talking to you, will sit down with the apostles to judge with them. Henceforth, see that you do not mistrust God in His servants." The young brother John immediately threw himself down at the feet of my father saying, "Forgive me father for I have sinned. I am now sure that the Holy Spirit is dwelling within you." After this they all left him glorifying God and amazed at what had happened.

It happened once that our father the prophet St. Shenouda went to the royal court, to the impious kings, because of the oppressions which the rulers were inflicting upon the poor. When he entered the city, the whole town was in a turmoil because of this visit to them. They were all coming to him, those from the palace and those from the whole city receiving his blessing with great faith and each and every one of them inviting him to their houses so that he would pray there. One day then, while he was walking, he met a noble man from the city and stopped to talk to him. The day had begun to decline and the time for the brothers with him to eat their food had passed. They were then complaining saying, "Our father will kill us by this hunger. We want to drink a little water." It was summertime and those who had been to Constantinople tell of the very high temperatures which often occur there. Our father St. Shenouda knew through the Holy Spirit dwelling in him what they were thinking. While he was walking with them along the street, he stopped, opened a door and entered, then asked the brethren to come in and eat. Upon entering the house, they found a well-prepared table with the same fashion as in their monastery's table with all their needs. There were two young monks standing there waiting to serve them in all their needs. So they said to the brothers, "Sit down and eat."

After leaving them, they said to my father, "Father, who prepared this table for us. Who were those two brothers who were serving us? Truly we would not find such service like this in our monastery." He said to them, "Give glory to God for He who sent food to Daniel in the lion's den is also

He who know, today, prepared this table for you. Those two brothers who served you are angels of the Lord." The brothers were amazed and glorified God and our father.

It happened that when our father St. Shenouda was sitting in the presence of the king, behold a noble who was held in high honour by the king came to my father wishing to receive his blessings. He greeted him and came to take his hand to kiss it. My father drew his hand back from him and would not give it to him. The king said to him, "My father, give him your blessing for he is a great man, both in the palace and in the whole region." Our father was saddened and said angrily, "Do you want me to give my hand to a man who defiles the temple of God with his abominable works?" Then the king was amazed and glorified God in His holy prophet St. Shenouda.

The king also sent us a meal consisting of some bread and a large fish, but my father signed the fish with the sign of the Cross and it came back to life. He thus sent it to the king saying, "According to our order, we do not eat these things." Then he sent a loaf of bread saying, "Place it on the fish and it will be cooked again so that we might eat from it." The king was so astonished and asked to bring my father to him quickly then said, "Truly, you are a saint of God living among people." The king then asked my father about their food and my father told him. The king answered, "Truly, your canons are good and your way of life is excellent." During his reign, the king was so charitable to the poor

because of our father St. Shenouda.

The king asked my father to pray for all of them, for their salvation. So my father said, "I will pray and you also have to pray." The king then gave him many gifts and he came back to us at the monastery dedicating Vesper Prayers for Wednesdays and Fridays for the comfort of the king's soul.

The Hope of Those Who Cry Unto Him

In the city of Akhmim there was a man who owed someone an amount of money. When the man could not pay, the rich man arrested, imprisoned and tortured him severely for many days to pay the debt. There was a person in the city that used to serve the prisoners. So the man sent his wife to him asking him to go to my father and ask for his interference to let the rich man release him from prison, telling him about the great distress and torture he was going through.

When she went she met his servant. As the mercy of God was dwelling in him, my father sent to the rich man asking him to release the imprisoned man so that the Lord may forgive him his sins on the Day of Judgment. When the wretched one (the servant) heard these words from my father he entered into the city and talked to the wife saying, "Here I am delivering a message from the holy man to release your husband. If you want me to take you to the rich man, you have to fulfil my desire first."

As she was a pure chaste woman she wept bitterly and said to that wretched servant, "Truly, I have never known anyone except my husband." She then went and informed her husband who said, "O my sister, you see the torture I am going through. Go and let the servant do whatever he wants." So she came back to the servant and said, "Do whatever you want on condition to release my husband."

He committed sin with the woman while she was in great despair. He then took her to the rich man and informed him about the message of my father to release the man so that the Lord may forgive him his sins. So the rich man released the man thanking God and St. Shenouda. Then this wretched servant came back to us in pride saying, "When the rich man heard your name my father, he released the man in debt." So my father sighed deeply because of what the immoral man had done with the chaste woman and asked him, "I wonder if you have taken your wages or not?" Then my father opened his mouth and said, "The Lord who had ordered the earth to open its mouth and it swallowed Dathan and Abiram in front of the children of Israel, may He also order the earth to swallow you now like them, O son of perdition." Before finishing his words, the earth was split and swallowed him before all the attendants who could only see the hair of his head while falling down to the bottom.

St. Shenouda Is Avenged

On another occasion my father arose and entered the city of Akhmim to chastise and rebuke a pagan man because of his injustice and oppression towards the poor. He warned him saying, "If you do not cease, the wrath of God will come upon you." This impious man who was a hypocrite and did not know God, stretched out his arm and slapped our father St. Shenouda on the face. Immediately, a very fearful person resembling the likes of a king, grabbed the beard of this pagan. He slapped him on his face and followed by a huge crowd, who came to see this fearful person, dragged him through the entire city. When they arrived at the river, the two of them dived into the sea and they both disappeared never to be seen again. Everyone who had seen them was sure that it was the power of God which He sent to take swift vengeance on the impious hypocrite and because of his many injustices which he inflicted.

Destroying The Idols

One day my father arose and went to the village of Benyot in order to destroy the idols which were there. When the idolaters came to know of this, they went and dug in the place which led to the village and buried their magic books in order to hinder him on the road and prevent him from reaching them. Our father St. Shenouda rode his donkey and when he began to ride down the road, as soon as he reached the spot where they buried the magic books, the donkey would stand still and dig to the ground. The servant hit the donkey to keep it walking but my father said to him, "Do not hit it for it knows what it is doing." Then the defiled magic books appeared and my father said to the servant, "Pick them up for truly we will hang them around the necks of these idolaters."

When he entered the village, the idolaters saw him and the servant with the magic books of which they buried. When they saw them, they immediately fled away and disappeared. My father entered the temple and destroyed the idols, one upon another.

He then went and preached to them for the salvation of their souls, but these cursed ones tried to hit my father and his companions, but the Lord strengthened the saintly fathers, until they pursued and conquered them. They then destroyed their temples and that place was called 'Biaha Elwaly' which means 'The Village of Grapes' where they used to commit grave iniquities. Thus my father burnt that place so that no one of these hypocrites might live anymore; as he had said for the glorification of God.

The rest of the idolaters of Akhmim and Benyot gathered and complained about my father to the Prince of Ensena who was looking after their defiled idols and temples, which my father had destroyed. He sent a messenger to my father, but when he approached, my father went under a vine and pleaded to the Lord to protect and strengthen him. So the angel of the Lord appeared to him saying, "Peace be to you, do not be afraid. Instead of standing on the ground and talking to the Prince, I will carry you on my wings while talking to him."

The next morning, they took him to Ensena where he stood before the court. All the citizens of Ensena gathered to watch because they knew that he was a saintly man and the Lord was with him. The Prince talked to him in arrogance and haughtiness, so immediately, the angel of the Lord took my father upwards. They were able to hear him talking from afar and thus they all screamed saying, "One is the God of our father St. Shenouda. After a long period of time, they lowered him slowly and then the people carried him on their shoulders and headed to the Church called 'The Church of Water'. Men, women, and children crowded asking for his blessing, thanking God, and our father St. Shenouda.

When he came back to us to the Monastery, he wrote the commentary about rebuking the idolaters and their idols saying: "The Lord thundered from heaven, And the Most High uttered His voice."

Many times my father used to tell me, "The Lord has favoured me with the life span of Moses the establisher of the Law – 120 years. But if you grieve me, I will pray that He takes me before completing these years."

The Adulterous Priest

There was an elder priest who came to my father asking to preach to him. He did not have a wife and was under the pressure of desire. My father warned him many times saying, "Go and get married and leave the service of priesthood because God does not accept offerings from an adulterer." It happened that there was a man and his wife who were dealing with rich people, but the leaders and governors took all their possessions and imprisoned the man. His wife came to that priest and said, "Now you have seen what they have done to us. I want you to come with me to our father Shenouda that he might have mercy on us and mediate to set my husband free."

This priest resembled the elders who accused Susanna the chaste. He conversed with this ignorant woman and agreed to have an evil relationship and they committed sin. Then they headed to my father who knew about it and said to the priest, "You did not come here for free?!" So my father interceded and the man was set free. Then the man came to my father with his wife and kissed his hands. The man said, "You have done a great mercy to us, because I fell sick after all what they had done to me in prison."

My father gave him alms and commanded him not to be angry or envy his wife because they did not bring her here void or for free. The man vowed and said, "My father, I do not have any intrigue in my heart."

Then the priest also came again to my father who said to him, "Stay away from priesthood until you get cleansed, otherwise, God will not give you more chances." But this priest kept committing sin with this woman for a year and they exceedingly indulged in iniquity. Then they came to my father and he accepted their repentance. Then he warned the priest again saying, "Beware of priesthood lest you should be burnt." Here he judged fairly about what would happen to them. He kept visiting them but they still practiced adultery together.

So one day many people were gathered together and there also was the priest and the woman. The stench of their sin was spreading everywhere. My father went out with the woman and we were following him, then he asked her, "How much did you give him today to bring you here?" but she denied. The priest also said, "I come with her here in divine love." So my father remembered the laws of the Lord given to Moses on Mount Sinai and he hit the ground with his rod so it was split and swallowed both of them alive. The people gathered were so frightened and ran away. My father said, "The angel of the Lord struck them with the rod which was in my hand and they have descended to eternal Hades because they did not listen." This rod is still here, and he had performed many miracles with it, like that of Moses at that time.

Not Scared By Death

The heretic bishops, priests and monks complained to the governor of Ensena about my father as he used to rebuke them many times and advise them to repent because he loved all the creation of God. They claimed that St. Shenouda had killed a man and a woman in one day. My father was not worried at all because he loved martyrdom so much and many times. He always asked the Lord for it, and also many times asked for the illness of Job.

My father -by the will of God- went to the governor of Akhmim followed by many rich men and nobles of the city who honoured him and were talking about him. The Commander was a strong mighty man who wanted to receive a bribe and set him free. As for the rich and noble men, they kept defending him saying that this man did not do anything deserving death. The Commander spoke to my father as if he was an outlaw and a killer saying, "Who are you to kill a man and a woman in one day?" My father answered, "Samuel spoke to God and so he killed Agag the king of Amalek, and it was considered righteousness for him. I have done the same and killed him. Now you can

109

do whatever you like to me." Immediately the governor decided to behead him, but when the executioner pulled out his sword, two illuminating angels came out of heaven in a bright cloud and took my father upwards. Everyone watching was astonished saying, "Truly these are miracles and wonders." Then the angels flew and brought him to us to the Monastery in the same hour and we all marvelled because of his gifts.

The Blessing of the Monastery

My father had told us may times, "What the Lord has done with Moses the Prophet on Mount Sinai He has also granted it to me here on Mount Athrib." He also said to me, "The Lord has walked through every inch of this Monastery while holding my hand. He who cannot go to Jerusalem to worship the Cross of our Lord Jesus Christ should come here and visit this Church full of angels, and I will intercede to the Lord on their behalf. He who comes and helps, I will give him his wages. As for the unjust who come to this place and defiles it, double woe for them because they cause heavy-heartedness to its dwellers."

Many times my father had seen the Lord Jesus Christ on the holy table breaking the Holy Mysteries with him. He was filled with the Holy Spirit, and our Lord Christ blessed this Monastery and all there in it. He said to my father, "This is indeed the holy Jerusalem, and it will never become weak."

Truly my father, every place witnessed your pure sayings, O saintly father; the righteous wise teacher of the universe who even specialized in theologies. Abba Kyrillos had read and meditated in your writings and witnessed saying, "Well done and well written, O righteous teacher." He also sent messages to all other nations under his authority saying, "Whenever St. Shenouda comes to your churches you should know that you are so lucky and gained a great grace. No bishops or priests should offer the Lamb, pray the Liturgy or address a sermon if he is here until he arrives and they should have his permission first because he is given this authority from heaven."

The Camel And Its Calf

Once some people came to my father heavy-hearted because their camel had given birth to a calf but she did not have milk to nurse him and so the calf was getting weak. They kissed his hands saying, "Do mercy to us and bless this camel. We want her to be strong as she is the source of our livelihood." Immediately, my father signed the Cross with his Eskeem on the camel saying, "I ask the Lord to make you grow and to save you." Then he took her calf and put it under her breast and said to her, "As you have given birth to him, let him nurse easily." So she did in front of its owners and they left greatly rejoiced.

The Island With Vineyards

On a later occasion there was an island in the western side of the river planted with vineyards. They called it 'the island of wind' and it laid in the region of the city of Akhmim. The owners of these vineyards were pagans who each year forced on the farmers the rotten wine of the island, taking from them by violence what was not theirs. These farmers arose and went to the monastery and complained to my father the prophet saying, "We have been suffering these great injustices for many years." My father said to them, "Arise and go. Soon God will solve the problem." During the night, our father St. Shenouda arose and went over to that island and struck the soil of the island with his rod which he used to lean on saying, "O island, I say to you, go in to the middle of the river and sink down forever so that the poor will cease to suffer because of you." Straight away the island with the vineyards went into the middle of river before the break of dawn. In this way the name of God was glorified by our holy father St. Shenouda the righteous.

His Patience

It happened one time that there was a feast day in the monastery in commemoration of our fathers. When some priests and chanters entered into the monastery, they came to my father and asked him for food, so he gave them what they needed. After this, they kept asking him for more and more and he gave them gladly. Again they kept asking insatiably and he continued to give them. Those who were sitting by were amazed by his generosity and patience and said, "As long as you are giving them they will not stop asking for more." St. Shenouda answered them, "They will keep eating and drinking only the things which are here for they have no hope of the next life. I am quite confident in God that they will never come back again." It happened that they died before going back.

St. Shenouda Rescues The Captives

It happened once that there was an atheist whose name was Gesious. He was very impious and hypocritical, speaking blasphemies against Christ. When my father heard of his profanities, he excommunicated him saying, "Your tongue shall be tied to your big toe in the bottom of Hell." This is what indeed happened to him after he died. My father testified to us and said, "I saw in Hades with his tongue tied to his big toe in great torture without mercy because of his impiousness."

It happened one time that the Blenges came and captured some of the cities and took captive the men and their beasts. With all that they had captured, they went and dwelt in the city of Epsoi. Then my father St. Shenouda wanted to go to them for the sake of the Christians who were captured. When he came close to them, those whom he met first raised their spears intending to kill him. Their hands immediately became stiff and dried up like wood and they couldn't move them and they cried out in great distress. The same thing happened to the rest of these people until my father arrived to the seat of their leader. When the leader realised that they could not overcome the power which was with him, he arose and bowed to the ground before him saying, "I beg and ask you to restore my men's hands and I will give you whatever you ask for." When he had made the sign of the Cross over them, their hands were immediately restored. When the king promised him gifts, he refused saying, "Only give me the men. Take for yourself the spoils." The king freely gave all of them to him and kept all the possessions.

He crossed over to the west bank of the water with them and brought them to the monastery. There were one thousand men apart from the women and children. He asked the brethren to serve them, seven doctors were curing their diseases and numerous surgeons performed operations to their wounds. He gave fifty thousand dirham as wages for the doctors and surgeons. Ninety four of them died and were buried in this monastery and fifty two children were born. The total expenses was twenty five thousand dirham including legumes and spices for cooking each week, one hundred and fifty measures of oil daily and nineteen measures of lentils. There were four furnaces operating for baking bread, eighteen-twenty loads daily from which the brethren were not supposed to eat, but rather to leave it to these people; in addition to the camels, cows, horses, donkeys and sheep which we looked after through the mercy of the Lord.

Thus we cared for all those who were taken as captives, as well as all the guests who come to attend the liturgies and the passers-by's, whom we used to give gold, paper, clothes, shoes, Manchester, shrouds for the dead, cattle, bread, wheat, seeds, vinegar, wine, eggs, cheese, pigeons, flour, sultanas, grapes, fruits...etc. - everything which the sick people needed. The total spent was around two hundred and sixty five thousand dirham, and the wheat eight thousand measures, two hundred quintal of oil, in addition to the vegetables and the radish, which was beyond counting. They spent three months at the monastery, then we sent them back to their country while they were giving thanks to God and to my father St. Shenouda.

The Prophets Visit The Monastery

It happened one day when the bell rang for evening prayers, and all were assembled in the church, someone else came in behind them and entered the church who was of an admirable appearance, dressed in a royal robe. When my father saw him, he approached him in awe and spoke to him with great reverence. He took his hand and led him up to the stand so that he would read. The man gave the reading sweetly and with great dignity and all who heard it enjoyed his nice tune and lovely tone. He read the psalm which said, "Behold! How good and how pleasant it is for brethren to dwell together in unity." He also recited calmly, "My soul exalts you and glorify the God of heavens", and "many nations will come from afar and offer oblations to God" and many other things. When he had finished the recitation, he walked into the sanctuary and disappeared. Some of the brothers then came and complained saying, "Could our father not find one of us to give the recitation apart from this layman whom he led up?" When our father knew their thoughts by the Spirit he openly revealed the mystery to them and said to them, "Believe me my brothers, the admirable man who very sweetly just gave the recitation is David the prophet and king, the father of Christ in the flesh. It was he who desired to read in our church and so our Lord granted him his wish." The brothers immediately rushed into the sanctuary thinking that they would find him and receive from him his blessings and teachings but they saw no one and were undeserving. Then they were amazed in the way which God had glorified our father the great prophet St. Shenouda.

One day Abba Mardarious came to visit our father St. Shenouda. A certain Epsaltos came with him and when they had come to the church to receive a blessing, the Epsaltos stood up to sing and said to my father, "I want to pray in your church until the end of the offering," So my father allowed him. The Epsaltos went on and on without understanding the mystery and sang beyond measure. The Abba Mardarious said to St. Shenouda, "It is the Holy Communions now, ask him to finish and put an end to his singing. My father replied, "Why are you concerned about him? Let him sing. Behold there is a choir of angels surrounding him and responding to him having Communion. Look there is the Prophet David standing by his side giving him the words which need to be said." Abba Mardarious was amazed by the Spirit of God which was in our father St. Shenouda.

The Epsaltos then said to my father, "I wish if you would allow me to stay here for a few days." So my father granted him his wish and he spent some days with us. When it was the blessed Sunday eve, our Lord Jesus Christ and His angels came and entered into the altar while he was talking with my righteous father. The angel of the Lord nudged the

Epsaltos in his side saying: "Our Lord Jesus is here today."

The bell for prayers then rang, so my father ordered that the Epsaltos, whose name was David, to chant. Thus he did so beautifully saying, "here that your appearance is Holy, O my God" also, "God stood among the assembly of gods." He then chanted the Psalm with a nice tune, while we were following and responding and enjoying his prayers. Our Lord Jesus Christ praised that Epsaltos for his good chanting infront of my father saying, "Well done, O teacher and father David". Then the Saviour ascended to heaven.

After the end of the prayers, my father was so happy and was full of rejoicing. He comforted the Epsaltos telling him, "The Teacher of teachers has said, 'Well done teacher David.'" The Epsaltos David then bowed in humbleness saying, "Truly, I have gained a great grace and won a wonderful share because of you. May the Lord fill you always with His blessings and on your holy place forever. May He comfort your heart concerning your children now and in the everlasting life."

A few days later he said to my father, "You acted with me in mercy." So my father answered "It was our pleasure to have you, you have done and said well". Then my father sent him back to his residence accompanied by some people.

It happened one day that our father St. Shenouda was walking with the great prophet Jeremiah. They passed by a brother who was lying down with his head covered while reciting the words of Jeremiah the prophet. Then the prophet Jeremiah stood over that brother and wept to the extent that his tears went down and wet the bedding of the brother. My father St. Shenouda immediately roused the brother saying, "Get up quickly. Do you know where these drops are coming from?" The brother said to him, "No my father but I suppose it rained." My father said to him openly, "These drops of water are not rain, they are the tears of the prophet Jeremiah. He wept so that you might not again read his prophecy while relaxing and without heartfelt ardent." The brother then said, "Forgive me my father for I am not worthy to see him." This brother was called Apasia.

Another time my father was walking with the prophet Ezekiel. One of the brothers was sitting by himself reading from his book. The prophet Ezekiel went to the brother and stood over him. The brother who was reading did not know this and my father St. Shenouda said to Ezekiel, "Come and be seated, why are you standing?" The prophet said to him, "Leave me for a while, I will not pass by this brother for his reading of my words truly strikes home and is enthusiastic and with awareness." They then passed by another brother who was sitting in the corner reading his prophecy as well as those of the 12 minor prophets. As often he would recite them, beginning each one in order, my father would see each one of the prophets he was reading, standing by the brother until he finished the reading. The prophets would then come and sit with my father and the prophet Ezekiel. When he came to the last book of Malachi he fell asleep as a result of the long labour of reading which he undertook, but the prophet Malachi did not cease from standing over him. Then the prophet Ezekiel said to my father, "Do wake the brother up so that he can finish the words of Malachi so that he too may come and sit with us." My father went and woke him saying, "Wake up my son so that the great Prophet may leave since you are withholding him." The brother arose and finished the reading and Malachi greeted his fellow prophets and they farewelled and departed from my father.

The Brothers Miss
An Opportunity With Christ

It happened once that our Saviour said to my father, "When your children the monks go today to eat, I will also come, eat with you and bless them so that all the food that is usually offered to them may be well pleasing to them. The Lord Christ came but my father did not ring the bell and prayed the group prayer as always. So we waited for a while and then the monks started mumbling and asked, "Who is this man that is the cause of the delay?" They all were looking at Him because of His countenance, beauty, and politeness then He left.

My father regretted it and was angry with them because of their murmuring. He spent a month without eating anything. So I accompanied the good elder Abba Bebnouda and we went to see him. We asked him while at the table together and we apologized saying that it was out of our ignorance and lack of knowledge, and that the devil had blinded their eyes. Then my father witnessed that the Saviour came to him at that night and comforted him with His sweet words, saying, "If your children the monks had not murmured, I would have filled their tables with endless goods on this day each year, which is the 7th of Baramudah when our Lord was incarnated in the womb of The Pure Virgin. I would have eaten with them on that day." When he said these words, we too regretted it so much because we had lost the opportunity of great comfort. Then my father said, "Let it be according to God's will."

An Act of Mercy

It happened once that a brother sinned in a certain matter, he was after all a man and there is no one without sin except God alone. My father dismissed him from the monastery in accordance with the rules. He went into the desert weeping in great misery. When he remembered God's mercies and compassion, he returned to the monastery and gave himself up to repentance saying, "O Lord God, compassionate lover of mankind who does not wish death for the sinner nor the destruction of the works of Your hands. If today You so move the heart of my father so that he forgives me of what I did, I will be sure to come to You in continuous purity and listen to his words, always pleasing him. While these words were still in his mouth, there appeared next to him and angel of the Lord who asked him, "My brother, why are you so disturbed?" The brother answered, "O you with an awesome countenance, I am distressed because my father has dismissed me today from the Monastery and I do not know what I shall do. I am despairing of my salvation. From this moment I have no hope in repentance. The angel said to him, "If your father accepted you back again, will you observe the vow you made with God and carry out to the full what you have just promised?" Straight away the brother fell at the feet of the angel and said, "Yes my lord. If his mercy falls on me, I will keep and fulfil my vows." When the angel appeared to the monk he was wearing the monastic attire as the brother later informed us. The angel said to him, "Arise and go to him and he will accept you." The brother said to the angel, "What if those on guard at the door prevent me from entering?" The angel said to him, "Get going now for you will find no one at the gate. Go in quickly and you will find your father sitting at the door of the entrance to the church. Say to him that he who was separated from you, who was just now talking to you on the right of the altar is asking that you accept me."

The brother was strengthened by these words and arose and went to the monastery. He did not find any guards at the door just as the angel had said to him. He went in and found my father sitting at the door of the entrance to the church. He said to him, "Have mercy on me and do not dismiss me for I am an orphan since my childhood. May the Lord preserve the sight of your eyes O my blessed father." He then informed him of all what the angel had told him so my father answered, "The Lord does not wish that any of us should go astray." While they were talking alone, one of the brethren came to ring the bell for prayers. As they were accustomed, they asked my father first before ringing the bell, so he said to him, "Take brother Shoura and let him dwell in his cell again." The brethren marvelled of my father's mercy and no one stopped him.

The Brother Who Foretold His Death

There was a brother called Daniel who was responsible for the cattle in the monastery. He was a hard-hearted, envious, and merciless person with the animals and people. Thus three brethren came and complained to my father three times. So he talked to them gently saying that he will calm him down. The brother Daniel loved my father so much, so when my father called him, he came humbly and kissed his hands and greeted the brethren. My father said to him, "O beloved Daniel, comfort your brethren's hearts for they came three times today asking me to talk to you to deal nicely with them, now be strengthened in the Lord." The brother answered, "Long live the Lord. O father, by your prayers, behold the death, which is awaiting those brothers, I also have a share in it." The brethren regretted and kissed my fathers' hand. He then comforted them and let them go while thanking God. Then in a certain year, there was a plague and these three brethren died. Then it happened that this brother Daniel was walking and a wall fell on him and so he died on the same day. My father assured us saying, "They bowed together to God on the same day. I saw them under the tree of Paradise as the brother had said to them that he will have a share in their death in great joy."

Do Not Disturb Him

It happened one year that the Nile River did not flood and my father St. Shenouda knew from God the hidden reason for it. He also revealed the matter to us with his tears weeping bitterly and said to us, "My brothers pray to God. I also will go to my dwelling place in the wilderness for the week so see that no one comes to me." Then after he had gone into the desert, someone arrived. On the fourth day of that week, the Prince came to the monastery wanting to receive a blessing from my father. He called me, Wissa, the disciple of our father and said to me, "I want to meet the holy man and receive his blessings." I replied, "He is not in this monastery but has gone into the inner desert." He said to me, "Go and call him for me" but the brethren told him that we cannot get him during this week for this was his wish.

So the Prince vowed, being a man of importance saying, "I will remain here with you and not leave this place until you call him to me so that I would have his blessings. When he kept insisting together with his companions we headed to my father in the wilderness. When we knocked he answered us after a long time and finally he came out and rebuked us and said, "Did I not say to you do not come nor trouble me this week?" So we said to him, "Forgive us our holy father. The Prince came to the monastery with his whole guard of soldiers and it was he forced us to come to you." He then informed us that the good and merciful God promised to raise the River Nile this year in abundance.

We rejoiced for his words and he came back with us to the Monastery. When the Prince saw him he was glad and greeted him. When he had received his blessings he said to him, "We want to fight the Barbarians, let your mercy surround us and grant me your leather girdle that I may wear it and defeat them." He blessed the Prince and gave him the girdle. When the Prince left, he forgot to wear the girdle and went to fight the Barbarians. The Barbarians were strong and killed many of his soldiers. The Prince then remembered to wear St. Shenouda's girdle and when he went back and wore it, he could defeat the Barbarians. He then looked up towards heaven and saw St. Shenouda above them in an illuminating cloud carrying a flaming sword killing the Barbarians without compassion, and so he destroyed them completely. Then the Prince came back to us thanking the Lord and our father the saint and gave us generous gifts, then he left.

The Two Sick Brothers

There were two brothers lying sick in the monastery. One of them was zealous and watched over himself carefully in obedience following the regulations of monasticism, the other was very negligent spending his days in vain pursuits. Now it happened that my father came to visit them, so he came to the negligent brother and said to him, "I can see that you are suffering and near to death. What do you think of yourself?" The brother replied, "Believe me my father, woe is me for I have never kept one of your commandments. I do not know how I will justify myself when I meet with the Lord." My father wondered and said, "Let it be according to God's will."

He also came to the zealous brother who was caring for the salvation of his soul, whose illness was not at all serious, and asked him with the same words. The brother answered, "Believe me my father, I was zealous in keeping all your commands to the best of my ability. If God is not merciful, I do not know what will happen to me."

Then my father pleaded to the Lord saying, "Through Your

mercy O God, take this zealous brother and leave this fig tree for me to repair so that it may come back to you whole." The Lord responded to his plea, so the very heavily sick brother was healed and the other departed. This negligent brother kept living in his negligence and recklessness and we all grieved for him. When it was summer time while the bakers were spreading the bread on the roof to dry up, some brethren were laying the mud and this brother came with them. He was walking slowly with the basket of mud, being lazy and reluctant, laughing and joking. My father grabbed him and threw him to the ground saying, "Stop these rebellion acts. I swapped you with the zealous brother and asked the Lord to keep you hoping to repent, and here you are, still living in negligence."

Brother Hercules lifted up his eyes shamefully towards my father saying, "I ask your fatherhood to give me another chance this time only and I believe in God that your heart will have mercy on me." He helped him to stand up and did not touch or hit him. I was so scared, interceded for him and told my father that he was about to kill him, but my father vouched that at the moment he threw him on the ground he saw an angel interceding for him and saying, "He is mine." The brother came back to God with great awe, sighs, and continuous tears for a month. He fell sick and was dying so my father visited and comforted him until he departed. My father said, "Brother Hercules has departed to God today, his life did not have any shortage or decrease.

The Fruit of Hidden Virtue

My father's body had changed because of his asceticism, patience and worship. It happened once that he asked for a fruit of apple which was not in season. At that time there was a brother called Maghnitos looking after the livestock of the Monastery. No one honoured him and he personally always humiliated himself. He only fasted the 40 holy days, and whatever he received, he would eat ait all while everyone saw him. This he would do before going out with the livestock to the farm, then he would eat nothing till the next day. The brethren complained so many times to my righteous father about him, but he kept calming them saying, "Beware to envy your brother, you eat once at lunch or dinner and he eats once early in the morning and eats nothing till the next day, it is the same, only one meal a day."

They used to come to my father many times complaining about brother Maghnitos, but he kept calming them saying, "My children, do not give the devil a chance to deceive you with vain dreams, he wants you to hate your brother. I have commanded you in the 9th rule not to believe dreams except the vision of the saints and the sign of the Cross."

This brother, without anyone knowing, used to worship in the wilderness as follows: in winter he would go down in the cold lake praying from night till sunrise. In summer he would dig in the sand, go down and stretch his arms in the shape of the Cross praying to the Lord. When he had heard the righteous asking for the fruit which was the apple, he could not find it in that place so he prayed to the Lord saying, "Guide me to that fruit to give it to my father to nourish him." So the angel of the Lord took him to Paradise and he later told us saying, "Many saints greeted me. Then the angel of the Lord showed him the fruit saying, "This is the fruit which your father asked for, take how many you like."

Then the angel brought him back to my father in great joy and he gave the fruit to my father. So my father kissed his head saying, "Today I am sure that you are a man of the Lord. Believe me my son, I have known the secret of this fruit and did not eat of it except today. From now on, no one will oppose you or boast with the dreams saying I have seen this and that. Those who follow the narrow way no one should reproach." Then my father discussed issues with him as a perfect and wise man, and he appointed another one to look after the livestock. Then my father took the seeds of the apples, signed them with the Cross and planted them in the soil and said three times, "Move and grow so that the brethren might eat of your fruits because you came from the fruits of the Paradise." Thus they called that spot 'the Moving' as my father had said 'move'. He then headed to the wilderness and left us to dig the well. We kept working for many days but did not find any water and we were saddened. Then we waited for a while and dug another well towards the east. When my father came to us, I saw him praying where he planted the seeds, so I approached him, kissed his hands and said, "O father, do not let our toil go in vain." So my father signed the well with the Cross and said, "The water will never decrease from you forever."

There was a person working with us who was unable to speak, so I asked my father on his behalf. He crossed his mouth with his Eskeem saying, "God who has created you will release your tongue to talk", and it was so. This person thanked God and said, "I thank You Lord forever!" The brethren had the blessings of my father in great joy, then my father wanted to go back to the wilderness so the angel took him while we were all watching until he reached the mountain. Glory be to God for the wonders, which He daily performed through my father. Then we finished with the wells happily and the Lord blessed the fruit of my father and the workers ate from it.

Then my father said to me, "When you go, give the brethren from the blessing" as he called the fruit 'the blessing of Paradise' but I went and forgot to go to the 'Moving'. Ten days later I needed to go to my father for a certain matter so he said to me gently, "Why did you not give the blessing to the brethren on the day when I asked you to do so?" So I bowed and said, "Forgive me father, I forgot. But as soon as I will go to the Monastery I will give it to them." My father smiled and said, "By the prayers of the saints, the blessing went back to heaven on the next day after I asked you to give them some." I bitterly wept and cursed forgetfulness and absentmindedness but he comforted me and said, "The decision of God is blessed forever."

Then my father vouched and said that whoever ate from it will never be struck with eye conjunctivitis forever, so I felt sorry and regretted not taking from the fruit.

Things Which Angels Desire To Look Into

One day our Lord Jesus Christ came to our father St. Shenouda and spoke to him, "Since your friends, the ascetics in the deserts are longing to see your sons in monasticism, behold they are coming to you tonight." My father assembled the senior brothers and the housemasters in the monastery and spoke to them saying, "There are some monks coming to us tonight. If they should come among you, see that no one among you or among the brethren speaks with them. Instead bow down your heads to them and receive their blessing, for they are truly holy men."

When the bell rang for Midnight Prayers and Praises, where it was winter and we were sitting in the cell praying, behold our father St. Shenouda came in and with him three glorious monks came in. When the brothers saw them they all arose and bowed to them. When they had received their blessings, the three men left and my father was walking with them. When it was morning we gathered to him and asked him, "Our father who were these honourable men who came to us last night. We have not seen such likeness. They walk with majesty and wisdom and their garments are glorious. They were different from other living men and were like angels of God."

My father answered and said, "Give glory to God my children for the gift we have received. These holy men who came to us were John the Baptist, Elijah the Tishbite and the other one was Elisha the Prophet his disciple. These great Prophets desired to see us at work while we are praying and praising in the cell and to participate with us. They asked God if they might do so and behold He sent them to you and thus the saying which is written "Things which angels desire to look into" has been fulfilled among you."

St. Shenouda Is Greeted By The Dead

It happened one day that our father St. Shenouda went north to visit his friend the prophet Abba John the hermit who was also called the 'carpenter'. He lived secluded in the desert and he used to lock himself in a small cell, talking to his visitors through a small window. To the north of the mountain there are martyrs laid, their bodies buried in the road. Every time he would travel on the road, these martyrs would come forth before him and greet him saying, "Welcome O beloved of God." Then they would walk with him with great gladness escorting him a long way and bestowing upon him great honour.

Whenever he wanted to go to Abba John, he would change his route lest perhaps he would burden the martyrs by them coming out and greeting him like before. So they used to put on luxury attire and come out and shout, "Bless us, our father the Archimandrite. Why did you change your route?" My father would gently answer, "Why do you trouble yourself to see a man of dust? May the Lord make me worthy of your blessing." Then the pious martyrs would say, "Even if you go far away from us for many miles we cannot contradict

145

the order of the Lord if your are passing by."

Many times too he spoke with our Lord Jesus Christ face to face. Again he would sometimes speak with the prophets, sometimes the apostles would appear and speak with him. All the saints would appear to him and comfort him. Sometimes the angels would appear to him and tell him what he should say, whether in comforting people or in reproving them.

Praying For The River Nile

It happened one time that our father St. Shenouda was in the cell in the wilderness and he delayed his return to the monastery because he was praying in those days for the River Nile to flood. The devil had told him that the River Nile would not rise on that year, so my father pleaded to the Lord saying, "Have mercy on us so that I, your poor people and the many cattle would survive, and do not let the words of this evil one come true." The Lord appeared to my father and said, "Peace be to you, O beloved man. What the devil has said is true, but because of your supplications and tears you will have water in your land to irrigate it, without the quantity ordered by my Father to be increased. We will have mercy on the people and the cattle and I will preserve the land to be filled with water so that your heart may be filled with peace."

He also gave us a command saying, "Let no one come and disturb me." So when something was needed for the monastery, we were afraid to send to him. Now there was a second in command, Abba Joseph the scribe whom we told saying, "Go up and tell our father of the matter and ask him what we should do." He obeyed and went up to our father in the desert. When he knocked on the door, he heard him talking to other people so he was afraid to approach him. After a while, my father called him saying, "Come in, Joseph. Do not stand outside anymore."

He entered and received his blessing. My father said to him, "Why did you stand outside?" So he answered humbly, "I thought you had the elders from the city so I did not want to enter until you permitted me." My father him and said "You must know Joseph I never talk to men in the wilderness except the angels, the prophets and the pure Apostles and martyrs. Nevertheless today you missed a great blessing because the 12 Apostles were here but now they have left. They came to comfort me, and the Lord had promised me to have rest and be satisfied this year." Then my father returned with Joseph and we all rejoiced.

Crossing The River Without A Ship

One day my father went to the city of Akhmim to destroy the idols in the house of a man called Gesius. So he mounted the mule together with two other brothers who also mounted on other donkeys, brother Youshab and Akhnoukh. During the night they went down to the river and by divine providence, they crossed the river without any ship or sailor and entered the city. When they came to that pagan man's door, the doors of the house opened immediately one after another. They broke all the idols into pieces and threw them in the river. Then again in the same way they returned back without ship or sailor. That night the animals with them did not make a noise nor did anybody say a word the whole night until they came back to the monastery glorifying God for everything.

Resisting Nestorius

It happened on one occasion that the fathers assembled in Ephesus to ex-communicate the impious Nestorius. The nobles of the country told the king that in Upper Egypt there was a righteous prophet man called St. Shenouda, who foresees issues before happening, so he said, "May be he is one of the angels", but they said, "actually he is a human like us and his fasting, prayer, vigil and politeness have reached the Lord." They sent to bring him with Abba Kyrillos of Alexandria. When they came, they went to the king and greeted him saying, "May the God of our fathers increase your glory, O you king, who loves God." Then the king ordered to let them enter the Church and sit on the chairs according to their orders. When they went into the church to set out the seats and to sit down, they set out in the middle of the assembly another seat and placed upon it the Holy Bible.

Nestorius then entered in pride, arrogance and without modesty, took the Bible and placed it on the floor, and sat on the chair. When my father saw what Nestorius had done, he leaped quickly to his feet with righteous anger in the midst of the fathers, took the Holy Bible and struck Nestorius' chest with it saying, "Do you want to put the Son of God on the floor and you sit on the chair?" In reply, the impious Nestorius said to my father, "What is your business with this assembly? You are not a priest nor a bishop, you are just an Archimandrite." My father replied and said to him, "God has prepared that I might come here to rebuke you for your hypocrisy and tyranny, and reveal your impiety. Why are you rejecting our Saviour's sufferings and pains, the Only Begotten Son, which He endured to save us from our sins? It is He who will soon punish you with a very swift punishment."

Immediately Nestorius fell off the chair to the ground and became crazy in the midst of the Assembly. There and then Abba Kyrillos stood up and kissed St. Shenouda's head. He took off his coat and placed it on St. Shenouda's shoulders. He girded him with his belt and gave him his stick in his hand and made him an Archimandrite. Everyone praised him saying in one voice: "Worthy, worthy, worthy is our father the Archimandrite. They went back to their houses after exiling Nestorius to Kom El Shuqaf.

After a few days, Abba Kyrillos departed and they presented his disciple Discorous to fill his position. Nestorius was sick unto death so he sent to my father saying, "Take my wealth and give it to the poor." My father said to him, "If you confess the One born of the Virgin you will gain what you want", but Nestorius refused to confess and so my father cursed him and his wealth. Immediately the angel of the Lord struck him, his tongue swelled, filling his mouth and he died. When they buried him, the ground did not accept him.

Abba Discorous & Abba Makar
Ask For Help

My father spent many days in humbling himself and suffering. Our Saviour came at night and comforted him and said, "Send your son with the other brethren to Bishop Makarious of Qaw to comfort him during his tribulation for he is in great distress." My father called me and said, "Hurry and take with you some strong brethren and go to St. Makar the Bishop, they are in the temple with his son Penodion and the pagans are ready to kill them." Then my father lifted his arms to heaven praying, "O Lord, who sent Archangel Raphael and protected Sofonius son of Tofir and looked after him in a foreign land, help them now. I ask you who was with Joshua the son of Nun at that time to strengthen you in your fight, through the power of the Lord, so and you will be successful."

We left according to his order and his holy blessings were with us. It happened that we were successful and came back quickly. Shortly there arose a persecution against the Church. The fathers Discorous the Patriarch and Bishop Makar of Qaw came to my father for his aid but he was sick, so they were greatly saddened. My father asked the Lord and the Archangel to reveal to him who was perfect among those saints, the Patriarch and Bishop Makar. Sunday eve, Archangel Michael brought to him Bishop Makar, and they kissed each other and talked for a long while. Bishop Makar said to my father, "I wish we had you with us to help us in the debate, there is none among us who is eloquent except Discorous of Alexandria."

My father answered, "I ask the Lord who saved Peter from the dangers of the sea and from drowning to save you with His Holy Hand. I know that Discorous is an experienced scholar like his father." Then he informed him that Nestorius has died and the ground did not accept him to be buried, he was still hanged in the air, and that was the third day after his horrible death. Immediately Archangel Michael came and carried Abba Makar to the palace court at dawn. Nobody knew about it except my father.

A Young Monk Returns To His Father

There was a young monk called 'Mokhles' who was faint hearted, bored and tedious. He was much obstructed by childish thoughts. Because he was being tormented he thought within his heart, "If my father comes to visit me I will go with him to the world." Our father knew his thoughts so he said to him, "Is it true if your father comes, you will go back with him to the world?" The young man smiled, then our father said to him, "Through the prayers of the saints, I will send you to your true Father so that you may have rest forever."

The young man fell sick on the same day my father had talked to him, so the brethren came asking my father, "Do you want to come and pray for him that he might get well as he is still a young lad?" Our father answered them saying, "What concern is he of yours. Leave him alone to go to the Lord lest his struggle and toil would go in vain." He departed on the Saturday and they buried him. My father gathered the brethren, talked and preached them, then said, "Behold today a pure righteous soul has reached God today. It will go without hindrance to the places of rest and nothing can stop it from kneeling in front of the holy veil." The brethren listened attentively and praised God. They prepared themselves to serve God patiently and unswervingly without boredom.

St. Shenouda Helps A Poor Man

There was a poor man living in the region of Akhmim who came to my father. He worked very hard day and night and could hardly earn his living. He came on a Saturday, as it was a custom that all the needy would come to my father on Saturdays to take a blessing from his pure hands. When my father saw that poor man, he knew his problem through the Spirit. They offered food for all who came and they all ate then slept. After a while, they woke up this congregation of the believers asking them to go to the house of God and have His Blessings, as there were hymns and praises every Sunday eve, as well as lighting the whole Church with candles and lanterns until the Holy Liturgy in the morning, where they would partake of the Holy Communion from my father, then he would offer them breakfast and grant them healing in peace.

The above mentioned man was called Luke, he kissed my father's hand and said: "Guide me to a job that I may earn my living, I have had enough suffering, myself, and my children, and we are always hungry because of lack of food. If you think I should just stay as I am, let it be according to God's will. Now I am ready for whatever you order me to do." The saint asked the Lord for his sake and he was informed what to do. He gathered some cucumber seeds, dipped them in the Lakan water in the church then gave them to the poor man saying, "Plant them anywhere in the field and look after them carefully. This will be for your living provided by the Lord, but make sure I also have a share in it."

The poor man went happily, planted the seeds and they were fruitful abundantly, the man sent the first-fruit of the watermelon and other plants to my father and he distributed them among the brethren. My father then took some of the water on the altar and gave it to the man saying, "Sprinkle it on the seeds." The man did so, and the production was plenty, so he sold it and gained much profit, which neither he nor his father had ever seen before, nor so, they became very rich.

Then he came to my father, greeted and kissed his hands saying: "Send me some carriages and camels to bring your share to the Monastery, through your prayers my father; the field's production is so much." My father headed with him to his house with his stick, where he saw the stores full of wheat and other grains and seeds, so the man said: "My father, have half of the grain which the Lord has given to us abundantly because of your pure prayers." My father answered, "I do not want anything my son. They are yours and your children's. I am sure through the blessing of the Lord that you will never need anything your whole life. Arise let us go to the fields."

The man followed my father who saw that the fields were late in giving forth production, so he touched them with the stick he was carrying in his hand and said, "I say to you, wake up and give production to this poor man." He then came back to us in the Monastery. It gave forth production like the first time and he was able to sell again and never needed anything until the day of his departure, thanking the Lord and our father the saint.

The Young Ravens That Cry Out

Another day when our father St. Shenouda was sitting, talking with some laymen, a crow settled above them and croaked down at them. Then one of the men sitting by my father looked up and said, "O crow, what is your tiding for us?" Our father sighed and said, "Oh that ignorance which prevails over the sons of men, 'there is none righteous, no not one'. How can this crow know this good news? Is the crow your Father's messenger? No my son, do not again put it in your heart to listen to this bird, it is only calling to the Lord to get its food. Have you not heard David the psalmist saying, "He gives to the beast its food, And to the young ravens that cry out?" For there are many men who take prophecy from the voices of birds and from the sun and the moon and all the stars, all these things are idolatrous and evil. Again there are many who put their trust in the princes of this world so that no evil will befall them. They themselves do not know that if God turns away His face from them, they could not stand for a single hour for it is written, 'Do not put your trust in princes, Nor in a son of man, in whom there is no help. His spirit departs, he returns to his earth; In that very day his plans perish. Happy is he who has the God of Jacob for his help, whose hope is in the

Lord his God.'

St. Shenouda Speaks With A Corpse

Once when our father was walking in the wilderness with our Saviour the Lord Jesus Christ. As they were walking together, they came upon a corpse cast out on the mountain. My father bowed himself to the Lord saying, "For many years I have been passing by this dead body lying here and I never knew its story." Our Lord Jesus Christ touched the corpse and it awoke. It woke as someone waking up from sleep and he bowed to the Saviour who asked him to tell His chosen Shenouda his life story. So the man said: "I was a glass-blower in Assuit working with colleague workers. We then went to Akhmim to live and work there. Few days later I fell sick and a few days later I died. So they laid me here and went on their way, because no one of them was my relative."

My father said to him, "Had the Saviour come into the world at that time?" The corpse answered, "Yes, we heard from those who passed by that a lady with a baby came to Ashmunin. Everything the child said would come to pass. He would raise the dead, He would cast out demons, He would make the lame walk, He would make the deaf hear,

He would make the dumb speak, He would cleanse lepers. He was performing every possible sign. When I heard these things I resolved in my heart to board a ship and go north and worship Him but worldly cares did not permit. When the corpse had said these things, it prostrated itself and worshiped the Saviour saying, "Let your mercy come upon me and do not let me be cast into the torments again. Woe is me that the womb of my mother was not my tomb before I descended into these terrible sufferings."

The Lord said to him, "Inasmuch as you have been worthy to see Me on this earth together with My servant St. Shenouda, I will give you a little relief. Lie down now so that mercy may come upon you and rest until the day of the true judgement." Straight away the corpse lay down just as it was at first. The Saviour took the hand of our father St. Shenouda and walked with him to the cell in the desert and they spoke of great mysteries between each other. After this the Lord ascended to the heavens amidst the praise of the angels.

The Prince Asks For Help

It happened on another occasion that a Prince came south to Upper Egypt to fight the Barbarians. When he arrived in front of the Monastery, he sent to my father saying, "Have compassion and come to me across the river so that I may greet you and receive your blessings lest I should come to you and cost you hospitality." The righteous went to him, and in the boat there were two fierce lions chained, not allowing anyone to go out of the boat. But when my father came closer to them, they bowed their heads and my father blessed them. The Prince and his entourage wondered and he said to my father, "Truly; you are a holy prophet. Please bless us from all your heart because we are going to fight the Barbarians." So he said to them, "Go in peace. You will conquer your enemies." And it was so and they glorified God and my father St. Shenouda.

The Idols Are Conquered

In the city of Akhmim there was a great copper idol erected in the market. When the devil saw that my father was preaching to the people coming to us about the Lord for the salvation of their souls he became furious and sent his evil soldiers to mislead the people and deviate them from the faith. Their leader came and entered inside this idol and addressed the crowd proudly saying: 'I am the angel of God, I came to protect your city.' Then the devils came and kept haunting the crowd, afflicting them with all kinds of illness and infirmities and telling them to go to the idol and it would heal them. Those who were brought to the idol were healed; and the devils were performing many magical deeds in the city, telling the people 'do not go again to this monk Shenouda for he is misleading you with his words.'

The people therefore rejected the church and stopped worshipping God, and followed the idol. Then the Archangel talked to my father while he was serving in the altar saying, "Peace be to you, O beloved man. Arise and go to the city of Akhmim and stop this defiance openly in front of everyone." So my father answered, "I will joyfully do whatever you order me." So the Archangel Gabriel said, "Take some brethren, go to the city of Akhmim and head towards the copper idol in the middle of the market which is endowed with great magic. Stand on your feet and pray and you will see the glory of God appearing instantly. I will walk in front of you to accomplish what I have ordered you from the Lord. Peace be with you. Do not be afraid."

After the morning prayers, my father did not linger. He took some honourable brethren and went towards the city. My father saw Archangel Gabriel in front of him in the form of a person so my father said to the brethren, "You go first and I will come later." Then he looked at the Archangel and welcomed him and he informed him what to do.

My father entered into the city disguised. He stood on the top of the idol and on top of all the crowd whilst being carried on the wings of Archangel Gabriel. The Archangel said to my father, "Do not fear it or its words, for it will not like to depart the idol. You find a way to bring out the devil, for the works of the Lord will be fulfilled by you, so that the citizens of the city will become sure that its works are magic and delusional and that there is nothing true about them. As soon as its weakness and feebleness are revealed, I will show you to the citizens of the country and they will see you. Do not be afraid of them for the Lord is with you. Ask for a carpenter to come and make a hole in the heel of the idol and say 'I order you, in the name of the Son of the Living Lord, Jesus Christ, to depart the idol'. Immediately I will pour great fire on it burning the whole place, so the devil will cry out 'Here we are coming out on account of the Son of God whom you worship'. Then he will appear to the crowd whom he has misled."

St. Shenouda stretched his arms in the shape of the Cross and said, "Listen to me, My Lord, when I call and plead You today for the sake of all the citizens of this city. Grant them a new tolerant heart and let them turn to You again like before. Shine on them with Your Generous Light, that is the holy faith in You, from which the deceiver has blinded their eyes." As he was saying these words while on top of the idol, they all marvelled because they could not see him but they could hear him. My father was also praying this Psalm, "Let God arise and all His enemies be scattered, let those who hate Him flee from Him, as smoke is driven away, so drive them away, as wax melts before the fire, so let the wicked perish at the presence of God."

As for the devil, which was hiding inside the idol, he could not bear the words of St. Shenouda. He started mumbling nonsense saying, "Go away Shenouda, you can never conquer me because I am stronger than you and I have resisted many hermits and won. I am the most powerful because I am Satan, the first of the creation." My father did not stop praying and said to the devil, "Be quiet you cursed plagued one. The Lord Jesus Christ has ordered me to persecute you and expel you from this city forever". All the attendants marvelled about the negotiations of the saint with the idol while not seeing anything, they all together said: "We ask you, our father, to be visible and bless our city, and we will do whatever you order us to do." Immediately the saint appeared and all the attendants saw him amidst them, so they cried out saying, "Help us our blessed father St. Shenouda. We have gone astray as sheep without a shepherd. Had it not been for your arrival, they would have swallowed us alive." My father motioned to them with his hand to be silent and said, "Hurry and get a carpenter." So they did and my father said to him, "I want you to make a hole in the heel of this idol" so the carpenter did according to the righteous' order.

Then my father hit the idol with his stick saying, "In the Name of the Crucified, I order you to get out and leave." Yet the devil did not want to go out saying, "I am not departing my house." Then my father hit him again and said, "The mountains tremble at the mention of the Name of Jesus Christ, who are you compared to them." Immediately he became like smoke while saying, "I will get out of it O Shenouda. I have suffered great torture because of you." Then his appearance was that like a tall giant black slave, so my father said, "Show yourself so that all the citizens of the city might see your weakness and disgrace." So the devil said, "Vow by the name of the Living God not to destroy me before my due time until I leave my father Satan, and then I will show myself and talk to you."

My father drew a circle around him lest he should escape. Then he appeared and all the attendants saw him and were so frightened. So my father said to him, "How dare you enter into this city and spread this great magic?" So the devil answered, "The citizens of this city loved charity, built churches and always came to your Monasteries. You were preaching them and encouraging love, almsgiving and going to church, they stopped doing evil and did good deeds and rejected my father's works and orders, and so, he ordered me to do so and mislead the people so that they might

reject your teachings and accept my will and contentment."
My father asked, "Where are your companions so that I
might expel them lest they should come back and mislead
the people again?" So the devil said: "I vow to you, by the
power of the Crucified, they fled at the day when you came
here and I was working by myself. Here you are, conquering
me with the authority given to you by God, the teacher of
everyone." My father said to him, "O evil resistant of the
power of my Lord Jesus Christ, His Gracious Father and the
Holy Spirit, you are to never mislead this people again."
The devil became like a pillar of smoke circling in the air
and it vanished as everyone was gazing.

My father entered the Church while the congregation was
following him. He preached to them and forbade them to
listen to the devil any more. Then my father came back to the
Monastery, we all glorified God and His saints. My father
affirmed to us saying, "Archangel Gabriel brought me to the
city and took me back without a ship, holding my right hand"

His Compassion And Generosity

There was once a heavy-hearted man who came and asked my father St. Shenouda, "Let your mercy be upon me, my father Shenouda, the Prophet who truly sees the Lord. A person has arrested my two sons because I owe him 140 dinar. If I am late, he will take them to his country and my toil in bringing them up will be in vain." My father was compassionate and appreciated his humility and he gave him the 140 dinar. The poor man gave the money to that person, and his sons were released in peace. Then they came, kissed my father's hand saying, "We thank God and your prayers O blessed saint because you released us." The nobles of the city also glorified the Lord who has bestowed His grace upon them, through the prayers of our father St. Shenouda, who kept mentioning his wonders until their death. May his prayers protect us. Amen.

St. Paul And The Loaf Of Bread

One day our father St. Shenouda was engaged in his worship at night and after he completed the worship, he rested for a little while and saw a divine vision which was sent by the Lord. He saw standing before him a man wholly filled with great glory. There was a great fragrance coming forth out of his girdle and his face shone with light like the sun. My father said to him, "Who are you my Lord, surrounded by this great glory?" The luminous figure replied, "I am Paul the apostle of Christ. Because you love charity and give alms to anyone who asks of you and keep all the commandments in all ways because of the love of God, behold the Lord has sent me to you to comfort you because of what you do for the poor and destitute.

He stayed talking with him like this until the morning when it was time to assemble in the church. The apostle then presented him with a loaf of bread and gave it to him after blessing it saying, "Take this loaf and put it in the bread store from which the brothers distribute the bread. Many holy men have blessed this loaf and even our Lord Jesus Christ Himself blessed it and made the sign of the Cross over it. Now be strengthened and fortified. Do not be afraid. The peace of God shall abide and remain in you forever." He then greeted him once more and went away from him. St. Shenouda arose from the vision and found the loaf of bread and he glorified God saying, "With praises I praise You, there is no limit for Your greatness, I cannot count Your good things which You grant me. Let the blessing and comfort be in Your holy house during all the days of my life. How shall I repay the Lord for all that He has done for me?" Straight away he headed to the room where they store the bread and secretly put the loaf in the store room.

He came to the Church thanking the Lord and we all saw his face shining like the angel of God. We prayed together then he went back to his cell. When it was time for handiwork, the bell rang so that each one would go to his work until evening. Temrinos, was appointed by my father to be responsible for the bread, he was a very humble charitable deacon, came to my father, kissed his hands and said: "My father, come and pray so that we can open another bread store and bring out what we need for those who come to us. There is little left in the one from which we are bringing in at the moment. My father said to him happily: "My son, Temrinos, take whatever until it is empty." So he said, "Forgive me my father, there is only one bag left, and I want you to bless it." My father said him, "Go and take this bag out and you will see the goodness of the Lord. Take some brethren with you to help you." He hurried and went as told by my father, and when the brethren had gathered to carry out what my father had ordered them to do, they waited for my father but he did not come, so Temrinos said, "Let us take the bag out as instructed by my father." When the brethren tried to open the door, they could not, so they said: "May be the Lord does not want to give us bread." My father knew what was happening, so he came saying: "Come, let us prepare the goodness given by the Lord, if not should not be enough, we will open another store room to take our needs."

When they had prayed, my father prayed and signed the door with the Cross saying: "The Lord who opened the gates for Peter, open this door with His Mighty Power." Immediately, the door was opened and we saw a big amount of bread which came and poured outside the room and filled up the doorway. The brethren and visitors kept eating from this bread for six months, calling this place 'the treasure of blessing' until this day.

The Charitable Monk

There was a monk who was a farmer called 'Ebsada'. He was experienced in planting trees and seeds. He was exceedingly generous and charitable and whoever asked him anything he would give, especially the needy brethren who were living in the mountain and cemeteries. He used to take legumes and fruits to the hermits living in the granaries. The other brethren complained about him to my father because of his excessive generosity and donations saying: "Ebsada the farmer is taking everything in the farm, we can't find our needs or give the visitors." My father St. Shenouda said to them, "If we have not run out of vegetables, he is guilty of no sin. Nevertheless we will go to him at daybreak and rebuke him. If we are in need, we will remove him from the garden. Charity is great, its doer will never become poor, and her children will never be needy forever." The saint knew that the blessing of the Lord was with this man at all times.

That night after my father had finished praying, he laid down for a little while. He saw in a vision a very beautiful woman whose whole body shone like the sun. She held the sun of Ebsada and spoke with him saying, "Do not be afraid and do not stop giving charity from the fruits of the garden to the needy; I am with you at all times, I am the Mother of human beings. I carried the joy of the whole world, Christ my beloved Son. He is the Giver of the fruits, He fills the wells and He gives strength to the animals. Behold I say to you, the heart of my Lord and my Son is satisfied with you because you give a few vegetables to the brothers and all who are in need." When my father heard these words from the Mother of God to Ebsada the farmer he was sure she was the Mother of Light. She then talked to my father saying: "Peace be to you Shenouda, O beloved of My Son. Behold I bring to you him whom they accuse before you. If you find in him any guilt, I will punish him with a serious illness."

My father marvelled of what he had seen and when the bell rang for the morning prayers at church, he went first to the Church and saw brother Ebsada praying while his ten fingers were shining like ten lamps. My father asked him, "Who are you whom I see like this?" So he said, "I am your son Ebsada." My father asked, "Who brought you here?" He said, "Certainly, the one who talked to you about me didn't hide anything from you my father." My father said to him, "It is written my son, 'Your God is the God of gods, the Lord of lords and King of kings.' I am sure now that the Lord is with you with whatever you are doing. Today I will come to you in the garden to visit you. Be charitable and merciful and never be disinclined."

On the third hour, my father secretly went to him in the garden. He saw him gathering vegetables for the brothers. Ebsada the farmer rose up and received the blessing of my father saying, "I have won a great blessing today because of your visit my father, I have faith in God and in your prayers that your blessing will be with us always." My father's heart was pleased with him and he greatly rejoiced and said, "I ask the Lord, to prolong His blessings on you and on your toil."

St. Shenouda then saw the Holy Virgin Mary with a bowl of water placed before her. She guide the hand of Ebsada to the bowl, sprinkled the water on the plants and legumes while saying, "Grow and multiply without toil." After that, she farewelled him in peace and left in great glory. Then my father St. Shenouda was sure that Ebsada was a pious righteous one, and that the Lord was with him in everything that he did.

Sickness Because of Sins

It happened one day that they brought a sick man who was a priest to my father to pray for him. The man was 80 years old. His whole body was swollen with many ulcers oozing, and he had diarrhoea. My father entered the altar and prayed, "O Lord, present in heaven and earth forever. Look at this sick brother and have mercy upon him according to Your will, for You are the Healer of all mankind. Glory be to You forever. Amen." When he finished praying, he heard a voice from heaven saying, "Be sure my beloved that is has been decided he will depart this body. Ask him about what he has done."

My father went out to the sick priest and said, "You have to know my son, that you have committed a great sin more than anyone else. Now tell me about your iniquities so that I may pray and plead on your behalf as it is written, "Confess your trespasses to one another that He may forgive you." The priest answered, "I have committed many sins." So my father answered, "Do not be shy for we are all sinners and all fall." As he was very sick, he sighed and said, "Woe to me my father! I have burdened myself with many iniquities more than anyone else. My father, I am telling you; I witnessed falsely against someone, I favoured the murderers, I ate and drank with the money of the Church's utensils which I sold. I used to commit adultery in the corners of the Church and next to the altar. I am wretched and miserable, more than anyone else." My father said to him, "Why didn't you fear God just for one day?" Then he called one of his friends who brought him and said, "Carry him and take him back to his house." And so he departed after two days.

The Nobleman Who Did Not Listen

There was a noble person called Hindious who was unjust. He loved the daughter of a poor man so he dismissed her father who had come to us, kissed my father's hands and who told him the story. My father sent a letter to that man warning him saying, "Let go of the daughter of that man and do not commit sin with her because you are not allowed to commit adultery with the daughter of that man." The noble man did not care about the letter of my father. Then the messenger came another time to us and my father said, "May the Lord decide concerning that poor man tonight, as it is written 'He will be delivered to Me to judge. Vengeance is Mine, I will repay, says the Lord.'"

That midnight, the Lord sent severe pain in the ears of the nobleman. He suffered a great deal and could not sleep or sit up, to the extent that he wanted to throw himself in the sea because of that severe pain. At morning, they carried him and brought him to the Monastery. My father did not allow to open the door for him saying, "The ignorant and unjust will all perish. Let him learn his lesson so that he might stop being unjust." When the brethren saw that he was in great pain, they pleaded to my father, "Have mercy on him because he has just now vowed not to object you all the days of his life." So my father allowed him to enter and he came and kissed my father's hands saying, "Have mercy on me, I am in severe pain, I will do whatever you order, I did not harm the girl for which you sent me the letter." My father was compassionate and prayed for him saying, "O Lord, You who takes away all the sins even though they are numerous like the sand of the sea. You who put Your hands on the ears of those before and they were healed and heard. You are the same, today and forever." Then my father signed him with the Cross. Immediately two worms came out of his ears and he was healed instantly. My father said to him, "Now you have been healed do not sin again lest a worse would happen to you." He returned home glorifying God and the St. Abba Shenouda.

The Blessing Of The Wheat

There came a time when the Monastery needed wheat. Now my father had said in his sweet words, "If the Lord gives something to the country we will have our share." My father gave me some dirham and sent me to the market, but they did not want to sell us anything or treat us kindly." My father sighed for Akhmim and cursed all those who asked for drought and famine.

Then he entered the church and prayed bitterly lifting his hands up to Heaven, "O God, do not reject us, look at our house and the other holy houses and to Your people who plead to you." We who were there, 20 of us, were responding, "Keryalison, O Lord Have Mercy." He kept praying for a long time while we were bowing and pleading God from all our hearts. Suddenly the doors of the Church were opened. I looked at the nave of the Church and it was bright as the afternoon sunshine, while it was night. I saw a huge amount of wheat and a number of saints standing in three rows stretching their arms in the shape of the Cross and praying. I was frightened because of my weakness. I went to the altar where my father and the brethren were while they were

187

bowing with their faces to the ground pleading the Lord. I went near my father and told him what I had seen. He was so happy, he looked at the brethren and asked them to stand up because of his compassion. They all went outside the Church and saw the blessing of the Lord and rejoiced. They glorified the Lord for His goodness. I approached my father, kissed his hands saying, "I want you to tell me the names of these saints who were standing next to the wheat." No one had seen those saints except my father Joseph the Scribe but the rest of the brethren only saw the wheat in the nave of the Church.

My father went to the middle door, he greeted them waving with his hand and they did the same in return. Then I kissed his hand for the second time and said, "Tell me the name of these saints. The adornment of them is well pleasing." After I was insisting, he started pointing to them one after the other saying, "The first one in this row is Anba Balamoun, the father of the region of Faw, this is Anba Pakhomios who talked to the Lord many times, and this is Tadros his disciple. This is Horesios called the 'Israelite' the equal to the angels. This is Abba Victor whom I accompanied to the Council and this is Youanis the owner of the Bakhanas cell, the lover of pure community. This is Anba Badronious who praised the Lord in his singing and this is Abba David, whom the Saviour had praised while visiting us saying, "Well done, David." This is Abba Akhrimon who judged according to the truth and this is Abba Fasarioun who kept the Councils and Laws' decisions. This is Abba Delmarious the seer of angels and this is Abba David who braided the ropes for the service of the brethren, and who inspected them." Then he started with the second row. They were the martyrs and said, "This handsome youth, is the prince Victor the son of Romanos. He is the father of martyrs." He then started mentioning those in the third row, and he showed me the Pure Virgin, the Mother of God and all those standing with her. He continued "This is Abba Bishay and Abba Pigol who dwelt among us with the power of his holiness and the love of God. Abba Bishay whose teeth were more precious than jewels. This is Abba Abgous my physical father. This is the pure elder priest Abba Bebnoudah who departed recently. They will come and meet you on the day of your departure"

Then I knelt and kissed his feet saying, "Truly you have shown great mercy to me today my pure father. May the Lord bless the day when I met you." Then he ordered us to close what the Lord had granted. So as soon as we went, the saints entered the altar and no one saw them except me. Then he ordered me to call the other brethren separately and we transformed the wheat before prayers, they never needed anymore till this day. They all glorified God and our father St. Shenouda.

Abba Thomas

At the mountain of Shenshif, there was a hermit called Abba Thomas who was loved by everyone. My father would say to me that no one was equal to him. Our Lord Jesus Christ had talked to him personally mouth to mouth. The angels had visited him many times and our Lord had led him to my father's place in the wilderness. The Lord also led my father to the dwelling of the righteous Abba Thomas on other occasions. He comforted both of them while being together many times.

When the day of his departure was close, he came to the wilderness and they both talked together on the wonders of God. Abba Thomas said to my father, "Today I will leave you. After a short while the Lord will take my soul. This is the last time I will talk to you in the body because the angel of the Lord has informed me last night. He has also informed me about the day of your departure. Let your children mark this date that it may be a sign for them till eternity, as it is the birthday of Abba Kyrillos the Wise and the Archbishop of Alexandria and Abba Victor the Archimandrite of Tabaneese, not only the same day but also the same hour. It is known and holy, it is the 7th of Abib; countless saints will come out to meet you."

My father asked, "How would I know the day of your departure?" Abba Thomas said to him, "I will tell you a wondrous event. The stone on which you sit on outside your cell seeing the sins of the whole world will split into two, it will be as if you are opening a book. The moment when my soul will depart my body, Archangel Raphael who guided Tobit the son of Tobias to a foreign land, you will see him walking in front of you. You will come to my dwelling place without a ship. Show me mercy for the sake of the Lord and bury my body for I am an orphan. I have no one except God alone; then it shall brought to me what was written, 'I will increase your blessing' and I am sure your heart will rest as well as those who come with you. May the Lord reward you for your charity and grant you His reward."

My father marvelled at the words of Abba Thomas. He then grieved for what the saint had said, "I shall soon die or rather I shall survive. Let it be according to God's will." Then the hermit Abba Thomas kissed my father's hand saying, "From today I entrust you to God until I meet you in the assembly of the saints." Then he left him and went back to his place.

My father gave himself up in his worships. After three months while my father was standing at the previously mentioned stone, he prayed and then sat down to have a little rest. The stone suddenly was split into two - it is a wonder till this day. My father grieved heartily and said, "Truly, Shenshif has lost its bright lantern of the wilderness,

Abba Thomas the Hermit." Then he saw Archangel Raphael pointing to him with his right hand saying, "Peace be to you, O friend of God and the beloved of all the chosen ones and the saints. Let us bury the body of the saint for the Lord and His angels are waiting for you."

He followed him and came to the Monastery at night. They met a fervent brother praying the Psalm "At midnight I will rise to give thanks to You, because of Your righteous judgments"; so my father said to him, "Follow me." Then they passed by another brother, Akhnoukh, who was praying the Psalm, "He shall cover you with His feathers, and under His wings you shall take refuge; His truth shall be your shield and buckler." My father said to him, "Follow me." Then they passed by the third one, Abba Yousab the wise scribe who was praying the Psalm, "They have bowed down and fallen, but we have risen and stand upright." So my father said to him, "Peace be to you, O good fruit, follow me."

He entered the altar and prayed with the three fervent brothers and then they followed Archangel Raphael who was walking in front of them until they reached the door of his cell without a ship. My father entered first while saying, "Bless me". He then heard David the Psalmist saying, "Blessed is He who comes in the Name of the Lord." He then played on his harps while chanting, "Our mouths are filled with joy." Then our Lord Jesus Christ ascended with His angels. My father called the brethren and they prayed for a long time. They shrouded and buried him in great honour, and then they went back to the Monastery without a ship. No one opened his mouth or said a word as Archangel

Raphael was walking in front of them holding a sceptre of fire.

This my beloved was what had happened. I am narrating it to you so that you may glorify the Lord and His saints. I have narrated to you the virtues and the wonders of our great St. Abba Shenouda; the founder of the Apostolic Law, the celibate, the Archimandrite, the priest, the equivalent of the angels, the good teacher, which God has performed by his hands. I saw them with my own eyes, I heard them with my own ears, and I touched them with my own hands, I, Wissa, the disciple of my pure elder father the saint. May his blessings be with us and with the writer of these words and all the children of baptism. Amen

Towards The End of His Life

My father became an old man. Towards the end he was bedridden close to his depart on the 1st of Abib. The Saviour came and comforted him, so my father said to Him, "My Lord and My God, is it possible that You might strengthen me like before to go to the Council because the Patriarch sent a messenger inviting me to defend the heresies against the Holy Trinity, as well as accusing You concerning Your Divinity?" The Lord answered gently, "My chosen Shenouda. Do you want more years on top of this age? You are 109 years and 2 months old. You wore the Eskeem at the age of nine. You have been a monk for 100 years and 2 months. On the blessed day of 7th of Abib you will come to me to have eternal rest. They will blaspheme on me at that Council just when Arius blasphemed on me. I appeared to St. Peter the Seal of Martyrs with my robe torn keeping fast hold of him so that he might not leave Me. Peter asked me, "Lord, who tore you robe?" I answered, "Arius did for he has separated Me from the Father and the Holy Spirit." My father St. Shenouda said, "I wish he was close to me for I would strike him with my rod, before stretching his hand to tear Your robe. Then I would have cut his tongue before blaspheming on You, the Creator of heaven and earth."

The Lord Jesus then said, "Blessed are you my chosen Shenouda. You will be granted goodness because you showed compassion for Me and my robe, my robe on which the Jews had casted a lot. When you depart, my angel will guide your disciple Wissa to bring them and put them on your body forever honouring you. Now appoint your disciple to be your successor for he is worthy and deserves it." After saying these words, He ascended into the heaven with great glory among the praise of the angels. These were the Saviour's words, which He said with His holy mouth to my father, who narrated it to us later.

When our father St. Shenouda was advanced in days, he began to grow ill on the first day of Abib. He then said to me, Wissa his disciple, "I would like a few boiled vegetables." I went quickly to the place where the visiting brothers eat and took him some to eat. He said to me, "Take it and put it on the roof until I ask for it." I did what he said. On the third day of his illness he said to me, "Go and bring me those few boiled vegetables." I brought them to him but when he opened his mouth, he found that they were off and stinking. He said to himself, "My soul you wanted this, now eat it." Afterwards he said to me, "Take it and throw it away" and he did not taste it.

My father continued to deteriorate badly until the 6th of Abib. We gathered all the elder monks who were present and said, "My beloved children, it is God's will that my soul will depart from my miserable body. From now on listen to your father Wissa, he will be your father and guide." With tears in my eyes and a broken heart I said to him, "Forgive me my father, I am not capable of this responsibility." So he answered, "It is our Lord who has appointed you as the father of the community and of the monks, so no one will resist you. May the Lord keep His blessings upon you and on His holy places forever. Be steadfast in peace all the days of our life, my son, and your body will be with mine. Beware of announcing the place of my burial lest my name would become worshipped. Bury it where you have heard me talking to the Lord Christ many times, in Jerusalem, the place where the Lord has prepared for me."

As for me, I fell on his chest and cried together with the brethren saying, "Are you departing and leaving us orphans, our father? Where would we find a person like you, caring for us, feeding us from both Divine and human food? Your sayings and sermons have filled the world. God has granted you numerous gifts." He said, "Keep my commandments which I have taught you and do not forget my teachings. Love the brethren, be charitable to the poor and strangers. Do not forbid them from visiting our holy monasteries. Accept everyone for the sake of Divine love so that the angels of the Lord might visit you. I will appear to you many times after departing my body as written in the Holy Bible, "I will not leave you orphans, I will come to you."

Our hearts were aching and when it was the dawn on the 7th Abib he was so sick. On the sixth hour I said to him, "My father, I am so sad for you, woe to me!" So my father answered, "The way is long and the road is harsh. There are terrible troubles on the way and mighty authorities. Woe to

197

me for I will meet the Lord." I said to him, "O anointed of the Lord, the head of our fathers. You gathered the monks in holy community; O you, mighty leader and lighting lantern for the entire world. Are you indeed also frightened after all the worship, struggle and numerous difficulties which you have performed?" My father replied, "With the Lord is mercy and salvation."

After he had said this, I kept silent for a while then he looked and called us saying, "Come my saintly fathers, bless me, and sit in front of me according to your order. The head of the fathers, the prophets, the apostles, the priests, the popes, the archimandrites, and all the righteous according to their ranks have come." Then he called, "My father Anthony the lover of strangers, my father Makarious the lover of humility and my father Pakhomius the fruitful tree, come to me together with your chosen children. My father Pigol who instituted the community for us, my father Bishay the courageous hermit, hold my hand so that I can bow to my Lord Jesus Christ whom I love from all my heart for He has come with His angels."

Immediately a sweet aroma filled the place and so my father delivered his soul between the hands of Christ and His angels on the 7th of Abib at the sixth hour. The brethren and I hugged him in tears and cried out saying, "Our carer in this monastery is taken from us, a great pillar in this monastery has fallen. We are deprived today of the bright light, who was looking after this holy places."

We then heard harmonious voices and singing of spiritual

songs above his pure body saying, "Peace to you O St. Shenouda for meeting the Lord of heavens. We rejoice with you today! You did not give the devil a chance to be present in your monastery during all the days of your life. Peace to you, O friend of God. The gates of heaven are opened for you for fulfilling the words, "This is the gate of the Lord through which the righteous shall enter." Upon hearing this, our hearts were strengthened and our souls were encouraged. We glorified the Lord as we now have a branch in Zion in the Heavenly Jerusalem. We shrouded him as usual and prayed on him in our monastery. I saw a luminous person guiding us to the chapters to read for him as appropriate. We all went to the cemetery, we buried him in great grief and agony and going back to the monastery around sunset on the 7th of Abib.

As for me, I ate ashes like bread and mingled my drink with weeping. I then took some brethren secretly, unearthed his body, took it, and buried him where he has appointed to us. No one knew about it except myself, Fr. Yousab the anchorite. Fr. Akhnoukh and Fr. Klistos as my father loved them. We placed him in a place from which he performed miracles and wonders. I had heard once our Lord Jesus Christ speaking to him at this place, which is Jerusalem, the place of angels. We mourned our father for 7 days while we were in great sorrow. He then came to me with other righteous saints, making me worthy to see them with him who were wearing luxurious attires.

I approached and bowed to each one of them. I kissed his head and pure hands saying, "you have put off my sackcloth and clothed me with gladness, that my glory may sing praise to You and not be silent, I will not be ashamed or dismayed.' My father said to me in great joy, "Christ has granted me many good things. He gave me an unperishable house, not made by human hands which is full of all goodness. He who listens to His orders and follows His commandments will dwell with Him. He also gave me a big house made of stone filled with all equipment's of torture, whoever disobeys me will be imprisoned inside it till the day of Judgment."

Then he raised up his hand and blessed me with his pure mouth together with all the brethren saying, "You will inherit the holy inheritance and all the goodness which I truly witnessed. My son, as the saints have blessed me you also will be blessed and your commemoration will be a great feast and a sweet aroma in this monastery forever."

After the saints had left, I called the brethren while glorifying God and said, "Truly God has given us a righteous leader and now my chaste brethren and pious fathers, we ask him from all our hearts to intercede on our behalf and ask the Lord to forgive us our numerous sins, and make us reach this day while we are healthy in body, spirit and soul, so that our Lord Christ might reign over all of us, partaking of His life-giving Body and Blood for the forgiveness of our sins through the prayers of my righteous father and all the saints."

Many of those who are deserving see him every year in his

commemoration.

Now I am to end my speech because it is time to partake of the holy offering. Let the brethren who came from a far place return back safely to their houses, through the blessings of St. Shenouda the Archimandrite, may the blessings of his prayers protect us all, Amen.

My brethren, do not be disbelievers of the struggle and the prophecy of my father lest great evil would come upon you. Also so that these words would be fulfilled, 'I have set him to be a leader of the believers, having the love of God in the hearts of those who call upon his name day and night.' May the prayers of our pure Lady the Virgin St. Mary the Mother of God, the intercessions of Archangel Michael as we have consecrated a Monastery in his name, and the intercessions of our father St. Shenouda be with us all."

We offer these pleadings through the grace of our Lord, God and Saviour Jesus Christ the Son of God. Glory be to Him and to His Gracious Father and the Life giving Holy Spirit now and forevermore. Amen.

The sayings about our great father St. Shenouda the Archimandrite has been completed in peace from the Lord. Amen.

The End.

www.ingramcontent.com/pod-product-compliance
Lightning Source LLC
Chambersburg PA
CBHW022128080426
42734CB00006B/276